The People's Choice

A History of Albany County In Art and Architecture

by

Allison P. Bennett

Sponsored by The Albany County Historical Association

Publication of this book was aided by a grant from the County of Albany.

Library of Congress Card Catalog No. 80-66320
Copyright © 1980 Allison P. Bennett
Third Printing October 1981

Printed by Lane Press of Albany, Inc.

Preface

Albany County has a dramatic history and cultural heritage that is worth remembering. The Dutch, who first settled here, gave their own particular flavor to the region. The people who came after them helped make Albany County the place of consequence that it is today. The story of the county has been in a large measure the history of the city and its place as the state capital. Also contributing to its prominence has been Albany County's location on the great thoroughfares of yesterday and today. The diverse forms of architecture within the county can be equated with some of America's foremost architects and designers. The quality of art and literature that was produced here touched national standards of renown. Many of the county's citizens secured far-reaching acclaim and the people of the county were nurtured by the general prosperity of the region and the intellectual climate that prevailed here. We live in a region of great scenic beauty, but much of the gentle pastoral countryside all too often has disappeared under the bulldozers of progress. Urbanization and modernization have destroyed much of the tangible evidence of our past and made it obscure to the casual observer. Often we must look objectively and search along the byways to find the meaningful bits of our history that are still visible.

Art and architecture are two of the tangible things still existing from our past. They can tell the story of our history to people of the present day. The purpose of this publication is to give to the lay reader an understanding of the significance of the county's history and to encourage people to look about them at the many forms of art and architecture that still remain with us. A concern and an appreciation for them may help preserve some of them from the ravages of progress. There is always the need to retain as much as possible of the visible evidence which tells the story of our history, and pass these resources down to future generations. Albany County will celebrate its 300th birthday in 1983. It is hoped that this book will be a source of inspiration and assistance to those who will be planning for an adequate commemoration of this event.

In pursuing this project, the author realized that Albany County has hundreds of fascinating buildings and architectural details, as well as many worthwhile pieces of art, which should be included in a work of this kind. However, the usual limitations of space and budget prohibited their inclusion. This is not to say that they are unworthy. In telling the county's story, an attempt was made to depict those art works and structures which best illustrated the style of their time and also were representative of every section of Albany County.

It is hoped that when you have finished reading this book, you will have a heightened sense of appreciation for the significance of the many events, personal attainments and the visual objects still remaining to us that indicate The People's Choice in Albany County.

Allison P. Bennett
Delmar, N.Y.
March 1980

Foreword

In an era of book titles which seem to promise a great deal more than the contents provide, the opposite phenomenon may anticipate a warm welcome on that count alone; this book will earn it on others as well. Those serious students of the minutiae of local temporal history will find their own treasure trove. So will the art historians, the aestheticians, the social and political scientists, the genealogists and scores of other specialists; but the special joys are those proffered to the generalist. In order to describe, in the most skeletal fashion, what Allison Bennett has accomplished here, it is necessary to understand the "state of the art" in the arts.

For a long time it was the fashion to criticise art in terms of elements extrinsic to itself. A work was conceived of as inextricably entwined with certain major elements of its time, or of times past, and of its creator. Thus, for instance, any discussion of classical Greek sculpture or architecture which did not linger upon certain general philosophical precepts of proportion, any discussion of Renaissance art which did not invoke Greek or Roman precursors, any discussion of a sonnet which did not explain the Petrarchan conventions which it was perceived to subsume, was regarded as incomplete, unscholarly and generally founded upon the quicksand of ignorance.

There came a time, in this century, when the pendulum swung the other way. A work of art, we all understood, must be able to stand upon its own two feet. What was important was *not* the artist's domestic life or the dubious critical canon of the era, but only what was contained within the four corners of the work itself. Whether it was good, mediocre or terrible, by any definition of any of those terms, was to be ascertained by examining the work itself, and *only* thus. All but universally this is still the canon, and one of its major corollaries is that it is possible to apply this canon and to explain and defend its application on a rational basis, with words.

Allison Bennett has corrected all this with a vengeance. Had this book been about some other area, one suspects that its impact might have been different than it is. One might suppose that a certain dour quality might emerge from the art and history of Edinburgh, a certain romantic quality from the art and history of Venice; what emerges from the art and history of Albany is uneasy apprehension of the slightly demented, which brings us to the book itself.

It is, first, a grand picture book. Here are pictures never before reproduced, along with very good contemporary photographs (taken for this book) of that which still survives. Here are miniatures blown up and maps shrunk down, all with impeccable captions. We are given pictures of churches, weather vanes, mills, bridges, barns, houses, and a lot of pictures of pictures, miniatures to murals, portraits to landscapes.

A number of these are demonstrably a bit crazed on their own account, but where this element is not obvious, the text comes to our rescue. It turns out that wherever the art appears to be conventional, the artist was substantially 'round the bend, and where both art and artist seem to have at least a tenuous connection with this earth, the subject of a portrait or at very least the owner or commissioner of the work was playing with something less than a full deck.

This effect appears to be related to a sort of galloping environmental senility, which is contagious. It is true that the book begins in 1630, but it promptly flashes back to 1614 and the trading post days, when Indians jogged into town with huge stacks of beaver pelts which they had acquired in the general area of Duluth, and jogged out again with something heavy or frivolous enough to make the return trip an exercise in pure madness.

Albany's claim to an inheritance of lunacy thus extends over three and a half centuries. Indeed, the founding Dutch had resigned in favor of the conquering English, who had in turn been ousted by the inhabitants themselves before the Louisiana Purchase was even contemplated. The City of Albany, which was chartered relatively late in the game, had elected its tenth Mayor by 1703. His portrait is here, of course. It is no coincidence that its present Mayor has held the office twice as long as the first ten together, setting a nation-wide tenure record; this book makes plain, such extremes are the norm in Albany.

Albany County, we learn, was already sending out missionaries to the West in the 18th century, the West being Syracuse, New York. You will meet in these pages such models of the conventional as the minister who preached the first Presbyterian sermons in half the towns in upstate New York, then converted and preached the first Episcopal sermons. You will meet (indeed, you will see) the inventor of the wooden pill box, the nationwide trade in which was the whole economy of another

Albany County hamlet. Here may be found the work of William Henry Brown, the incredible scissor silhouettist, who warmed up on a likeness of Lafayette as prelude to room-length silhouettes of funeral processions and fire brigades, so accurate that each mourner and fireman is identifiable. Here also is the Watervliet Arsenal's prefabricated iron building, the severity of the cast iron walls, ceilings and floors of which is relieved only by the material used for the exterior stair cases — *wrought* iron. Here are the Shakers, whose local presence was initiated with the purchase of two hundred acres of swamp.

And here, in glorious profusion, are the great artists and subjects. Here is Ezra Ames, whose early talents ran to the decoration of buckets, with a portrait of Eliphalet Nott, President of Union College for a scant 62 years. Here is Joseph Henry, who, nurtured in Albany weather, fled to Washington to found the U.S. Weather Bureau. Here is H. H. Richardson's neo-Romanesque Senate Chamber, all polished and shining like a good deed in a naughty world. And naughty enough it was; Albany was the capital, by 1797, of the richest and most powerful state in the Union, when Washington was a woodlot; Tammany began here. So also did the career of William M. Hart, decorating window shades; that of Timothy A. Gladding, painting houses; that of Homer Dodge Martin, whose formal training consisted in its entirety of two weeks study with the aforesaid Hart; that of George H. Boughton, whose best work seems to have antedated his seventeenth birthday; that of Asa Weston Twitchell, the demand for whose services may be apprehended by his two greatest claims to fame: a self-portrait, and a sort of club he seems to have run for other busy artists.

And this only scratches the surface, so to speak. The grand anecdote of the pencilled additions to the painting of the steamboat collision is worth its own book. Consider the tremendous frescoe in the Assembly chamber, portraying the Darkness of Ignorance Fleeing Before the Light of Civilization, which completely disappeared owing to the artist's ignorance of the need to waterproof a stone wall for a mural.

Here are the folk-art children who look like taxidermist's monkeys, the "mourning" art (not unlike the funerary verse in the daily papers), the dutch doors, even "hatchments", and enough of the truly great (the Ten Broeck Mansion, for one) to remind us that Albany was also the Albany of Herman Melville; the James Gang (in this case philosopher William and author Henry, although grandfather William appears to have resembled Jesse in most important respects); Alexander Hamilton (a native son-in-law); predictably, Aaron Burr; and a gaggle of Presidents of the United States. But just as the glories of the Hudson River school unfold, along come the houses made of cobblestones, to illustrate once again the slimness of the line (if there be one at all) between genius and madness. Perhaps the only difference between Albany and the rest of the world is where that line is drawn, and the fact that, in Albany, the line is curved.

Charles S. Woolsey
President,
Albany County
Historical Association

Acknowledgements

The preparation of this book would have been impossible without the aid of many people, both in and outside of Albany County. My heartfelt thanks is extended to all of them and especially to Charles S. Woolsey, President, James M. Flavin, Constance Gorman and William R. Wands, of the Albany County Historical Association.

My sincere appreciation goes to Erastus Corning II, Mayor of the City of Albany, and to James J. Coyne, Albany County Executive, and Thomas G. Clingan, for their support and encouragement.

Researchers and historians who have been especially helpful are: Fred Abele, Robert W. Arnold III, Thomas H. Blaisdell, Harold Colbeth, Arthur B. Gregg, Alice Gurney, John J. McEneney, Martha D. Noble, Jean Olton, Rachel Ormsbee, Paul Richmond, Mary Rudebush, Freida Saddlemire, Euretha Stapleton, Kenneth and Katherine Storms, Helen Strassner and Marvin C. Wolfe.

Grateful appreciation for their outstanding patience and cooperation is given to members of the Albany Institute library and research staff: Tammis Groft, James Hobin, Louise LaPlante, Kenneth McFarland, Charlotte Wilcoxen, and to the Director, Norman S. Rice.

Many people have graciously permitted me to photograph their homes and possessions and have made available pertinent information that was requested. I am indebted especially to the following: H. G. Abbott, Anthony and Edith Blaisdell, Douglas Boucher, Jack Boucher, Sister Nancy Boyle, Mrs. Charles Canestrari, Barbara Carkner, Mr. and Mrs. Jay Clemmer, Dorothy H. Cooke, Mrs. George Cooley, Frances Crounse, Daniel and Elizabeth Dryden, Robert and Lorena Embler, Edward C. Farrell, Edward Giddings, Maureen D. Gour, Dorothy C. Kellogg, Mrs. David Kunz, John Kusano, Richard Landers, Irving Leonard, Walter Littell, Josephine Loucks, Nancy Lynk, Robin Michel, Eveline Olson, Eugene Parks, Walter Pearson, William Pillsbury, Barbara Ruch, Hazel Ryder, Josephine Slingerland, William W. Shuster, Ernestine Taylor, Mr. and Mrs. Peter G. D. Ten Eyck, Carl and Lois Touhey, Fred and Jeanne Van Hoesen, Charles and Virginia Waldenmaier and Ella Willsey.

A very special acknowledgement of thanks must be extended to the person who encouraged the writing of this book, Dr. Roderic H. Blackburn, Assistant Director of the Albany Institute of History and Art. His inspiration and continuing assistance and encouragement was of immeasurable help to me and I am truly grateful. Also, I would like to give thanks to Roderic Blackburn and Charlotte Wilcoxen for copy editing and to Nathaniel Boynton, Jane Feisthamel and Arthur Gresen for special assistance.

I would also like to extend recognition to my husband, William D. Bennett, for his unfailing patience and generosity over many months.

Allison P. Bennett

Photo Credits:

Allison Bennett, Harry Bigelman, Roderic Blackburn, J. Wallace Campbell, Franklyn Dillon, Kenneth Hay, Robert P. Keough, William Knorr, Robert Riccardo, Marvin Sontz, Harry Thayer, Kurt Uhl and E. M. Weil.

Cover photo: Kenneth M. Hay

Table of Contents

Preface ... iii
Foreword ... v
Acknowledgements ... vii
Photo Credits ... vii

CHAPTER I Echoes From The Past - A Dutch Heritage c. 1630 — 1785 ... 1
   Dutch Settlers of Albany County ... 4
   Dutch Colonial Architecture ... 10
   A Brighter Destiny ... 18
   English Georgian Influences ... 20
   Aspirations Toward Elegance ... 26
   Patriots Of The New Country ... 28

CHAPTER II A New Dawn for Albany County 1785 — ca. 1830 ... 31
   In The Federal Style ... 35
   Mills and Manufacturing ... 47
   Weapons Of War From Watervliet ... 55
   Communal Living - The Watervliet Shakers ... 56
   A Crossroad Of Commerce - Banks and Bankers ... 59
   Portrait Painter Of Albany ... 61
   Folk Perspectives In Art ... 66
   Educational Endeavors ... 70
   The Political Perspective ... 72

CHAPTER III Coming Of Age In Albany County ca. 1830 — 1900 ... 77
   Anti-Rentism — The Last Patroon ... 79
   Greek Temples In Dutch Towns ... 82
   Titans Of The Age ... 90
   Purveyors Of The News ... 96
   A Passing Fancy — Victorianism In Architecture ... 98
   The Halls Of Academe ... 111
   Summer At The Boarding House And On The River ... 112
   Art For Adornment ... 114
   The Art Of Everyday Life ... 125
   Campaigns On Capitol Hill ... 129
   A President Passes ... 131

Bibliography ... 133

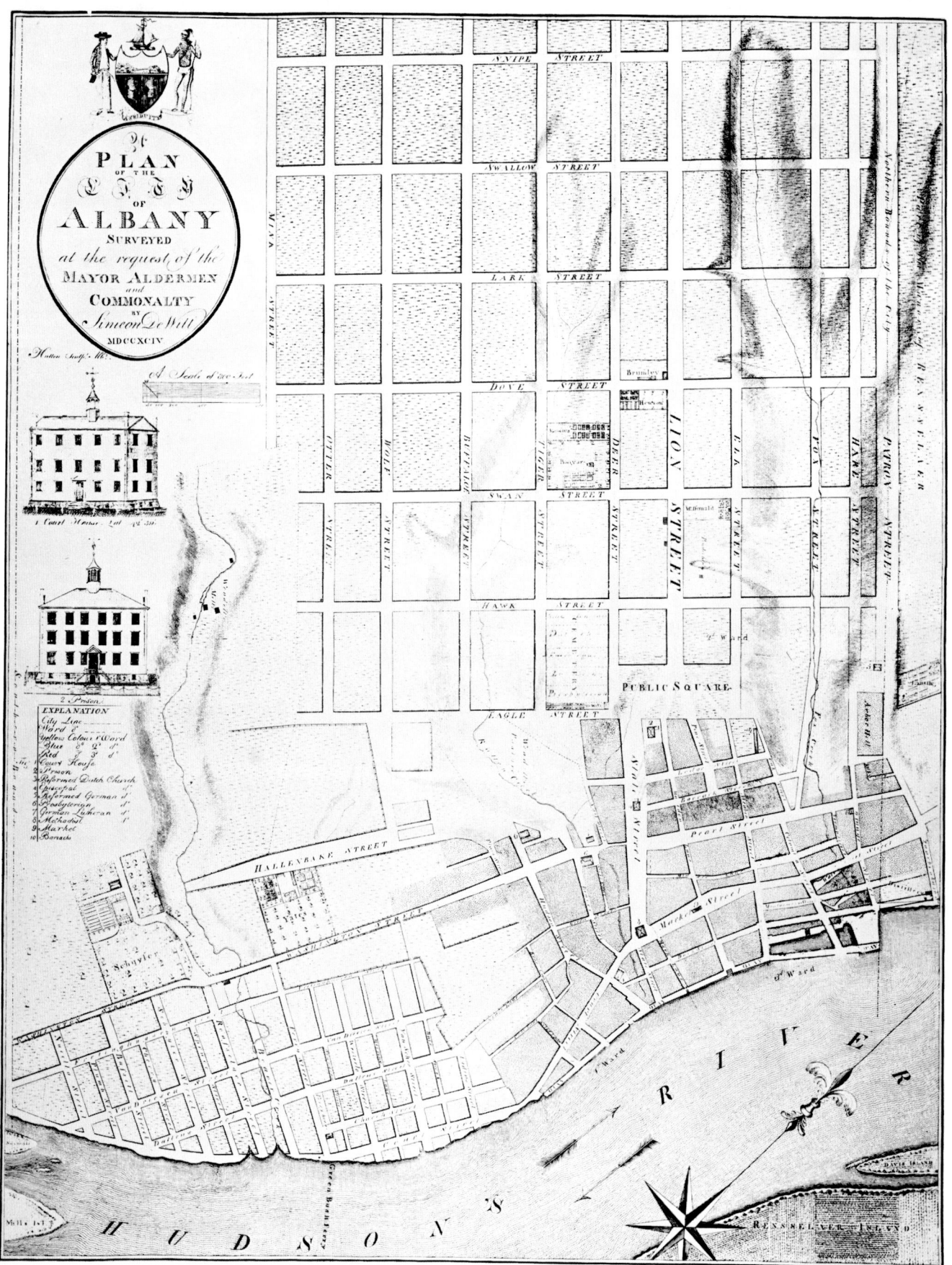

Plan of the City of Albany by Simeon DeWitt (1794). Courtesy, New York State Library.

CHAPTER I

Echoes from the Past - A Dutch Heritage c. 1630-1785

The majestic Hudson River often has been termed "Gateway to a Continent". It is the first link in a chain of watery highways to the interior parts of our nation. Since earliest times the river has been a dominant force in shaping the story of Albany County, and forms its eastern boundary. Its discovery by Henry Hudson in 1609 was the beginning of the white man's settlement in this part of the New World.

Albany County is situated on the western bank of the river, approximately 150 miles from the Atlantic Ocean, and it lies at the head of tide water and navigation. There is a great diversity to the land surface, with rich alluvial flats sloping into gentle hills, culminating in the Helderberg escarpment on the west. These steep Helderberg hills are a leading feature of the county because of their scenic beauty and geological structure. Beyond this, the land again slopes gradually west and south to the county boundaries, and here there are spectacular views of the neighboring Catskill Mountains. On the northern edge of the county, along the Mohawk River, the land is broken by hills and plains of clay and sand. The Cohoes Falls on the Mohawk, a drop of over 70 feet, is a well-known natural phenomenon of great beauty.

Before the coming of the white man, the Mahican Indians of the Algonkian language group lived here and farmed little patches of ground, cleared from the encompassing forest. To supplement their agriculture, they hunted and fished, and lived in bark house villages at several places along the river shores. One of their meeting places and trading centers was at the mouth of the creek called *Tawasentha*, just south of the present city of Albany. With the coming of the Europeans in the 17th century, these people already were sinking into oblivion, decimated by constant wars with the Mohawks on the west.

There is a distinct possibility that Frenchmen were here and trading with these Indians some time before Henry Hudson came up the river on his ship *The Half Moon*. However, he is the one credited with discovery, and, on the strength of his explorations for the Dutch government, the land was promptly annexed and the province was given the name *New Netherland*. Originally, this included a large territory extending roughly from central Connecticut to the wilderness lands north of Albany, and bounded on the south and west by the Delaware River as far as New Castle, Delaware. Situated as it was between the English colonies of New England and Virginia, the colony's position was precarious from the beginning.

By 1614, a trading post had been set up by the enterprising Hollanders, on Castle Island, just below present-day Albany. Here a lucrative trade in beaver and otter skins was carried on with the Indians by the Dutch West India Company. These Indians had already developed a modest exchange of goods among themselves before the traders came, partially because of the waterway system near which they lived. The tribes quickly recognized and eagerly accepted the white man's invitation to exchange pelts for European manufactured goods. One early historian gives a description of the ancient Indian trade route: "When the Dutchmen set their first posts up the river (at Albany) they commanded the end of the great Iroquois trail, a path about 15 inches wide, beaten hard by Indian feet, running through the forest, and everywhere avoiding wet as well as open places, which led up the Mohawk Valley and beyond it to a point just above Niagara Falls ... bands of savages from regions as distant as the further shores of Lake Superior easily brought their packs of pelts to the shores of the Great River" (Hudson).[1]

The Company's primary interest in the province was the profit gleaned from the fur trade, but fur traders tend to be transient fortune-seekers, and by 1629 it was felt that a more stable settlement would be needed if the colony was to survive and increase. In that year, the Company inaugurated a plan whereby manorial rights, including large grants of land, would be conferred on those who obligated themselves to colonize the new country, with the accompanying title of *Patroon*. A considerable area of what is now the eastern part of New York was settled under this system, and part of it was the large tract which became known as *Rensselaerswyck*. Kiliaen Van Rensselaer, a director of the Company, was given a grant of land in the vicinity of Fort Orange, near Castle Island. He purchased from the Indians, through his agents, a tract of land which eventually comprised about 700,000 acres. This included practically all of present day Albany County, as well as a section on the east side of the river that is now a portion of Rensselaer County, and, at a later date, some sections of Columbia County. By the early 1630's, the first settlers were sent over from Holland, to engage in agriculture as tenant farmers on the lands of the Patroon. Fertile farmlands along the river were taken up quickly. Later settlers had to clear the dense woodlands along the banks of the streams. Nevertheless, the fur trade was the thing pursued with the most vigor.

The fashion for furs did not diminish in Europe, and as the Dutch settlements prospered, the English from the New England colonies began making encroachments on the eastern borders of Dutch territory, desiring for themselves trading profits and also better farmland. For years the English had disputed the Dutch claims to the Hudson River areas, attempting to substantiate territorial claims based on the discovery of North America by the Cabots, with unlimited inland extension. From this, there arose ill feeling on both sides as to defined boundaries and privileges. In 1664, Charles II of England, desiring to end forever Dutch commercial rivalry, sent a fleet of ships out from England with the express purpose of taking possession of New Netherland and reducing its inhabitants to obedience. Governor Pieter Stuyvesant knew the colony was practically defenseless against an invasion and had no choice but to surrender to the English demands. British soldiers now occupied Fort Orange, and the town's name was changed to Albany, in honor of the English Duke of York and Albany, who became King James II of England in 1685.

After the surrender, the Van Rensselaers and other Dutch landholders petitioned the English government for security of their holdings. A new charter eventually was granted to the Patroon, in 1685, confirming again the relations between landlord and tenant. The Dutch title of *Patroon* was changed to the English term, *Lord of the Manor,* but the use of the word Patroon was carried on colloquially until 1839. The new Assembly divided the colony into 12 counties, one of which was Albany County. In these early years, the county was of great size because it contained all of what are the present counties of Columbia, Greene, Rensselaer and Schenectady.

The Patroon long had exercised a claim that Fort Orange was a part of the Colony of Rensselaerswyck. The Dutch West India Company had felt that it held the sole authority over Fort Orange, since it had built and garrisoned the fort 15 years before the founding of Rensselaerswyck. There was protracted dispute over the fort and the area surrounding it, but in 1686 the city of Albany received its charter from Governor Thomas Dongan, setting it outside the jurisdiction of the Manor of Rensselaerswyck.

The French in Canada were inspired with the same desire for furs and conquest in the New World as the English, and were eager to gain the allegiance of the Indians. In 1671, Courcelles, Governor in Canada, wrote "the Iroquois trade scarcely any with us, but carry all their peltries to New Netherland ... some means were sought a long time ago, to prevent the Iroquois going to New Netherland to trade."[2] There was a high feeling against the Dutch and the English for their encroachments on French territory in pursuit of the fur trade, for much of this beaver was trapped on land in Canada, subject to the King of France.

Four wars between England and France, from 1680 to 1763, had their effects on life in Albany County. With the French settled in Canada, the people of Albany County lived in dread of French conquest. Since Albany was the northern frontier trading town, it became the chief place of strength and defense against the French and Indians. It was garrisoned by a small company of militia and English soldiers. A crude fort, surrounded by palisades, was erected to protect the city. By 1756, the French and Indian Wars had begun because of disagreements over French control of the Ohio River region. Even though that territory was miles away, the effect it had on Albany County was quite conclusive. For nine years, the county was the center of military activity, with expeditions to the north commencing here, and provisions of every sort stored here for distribution to the armies. There were many complaints that the Dutchmen of Albany County were more concerned with their farms than with making war, and were so devoted to their own profit that the army suppliers found it a very difficult place. Participation in the French and Indian War did give the colonists experience in military arts and knowledge of British military organization that would be of considerable use to them in a few short years.

From 1763 until the eve of the Revolutionary War, Albany County was at peace. An influx of new settlers came from Scotland, Ireland,

Germany and Scandinavia, bringing new vitality to the region. Even so, Dutch customs and language were slow to be laid to rest. Restrictions on colonial trade and objections to heavy taxation by the English Parliament brought dissension into the area. At no time before 1775, however, was total independence from England considered a real possibility. The stolid Dutchmen preferred to wait and see if the unpleasantness could not be settled by means other than actual war. Nevertheless, there was a positive though almost unconscious movement swelling among the populace for real independence, influenced to a great degree by the Sons of Liberty, merchants who opposed tariffs, and concerned citizen committees.

The events at Lexington and the publication in early 1776 of Thomas Paine's *Common Sense* had an enormous effect on public opinion. The Declaration of Independence closed the door to reconciliation with England and forced everyone to take a stand. Albany County raised 17 companies of militia that served in the Revolution, and many of its citizens also served in the 1st and 2nd N.Y. Regiments of the Continental Line. Yet, almost half of the population of New York was Loyalist and Albany County was considered a nest of Tories. Even the mayor, Abraham C. Cuyler, sympathized with the Royal Cause. The defeat of Burgoyne at Saratoga in 1777 was the turning point and many Loyalist families left at that time for Canada.

During the Revolution, Albany again became a center of military operations, this time for the northern division of the Continental Army. The strategic importance of the Hudson River Valley made it a key in British plans for conquest. With the imminence of battles nearby and a host of soldiers quartered on the populace of Albany County, its citizens often were filled with alarm. They were asked to contribute money, food, clothing and ammunition to assist the northern department of the Army, and were paid in depreciated paper money. People on the farms were implored to raise more hemp, flax, wheat and sheep. Special committees scoured the county and state for horses, blankets, shoes and clothing. Even lead window mullions and pewter dishes were melted down for lead bullets. The latter part of the war was a period of great economic distress within the county. With the coming of peace, the people of Albany County were confronted with new problems. They set to work to restock their depleted farmsteads and mercantile establishments, and to rebuild their neglected trade and commerce.

Near the close of the 18th century, thousands of untouched acres of land in the hilly western sections of the county were opened up for settlement. People from the New England seaboard towns were lured by land hunger to the unsettled regions of Albany County, and crossed the Hudson River on ferry boats. By horse and wagon, they went over dirt paths to take up 120-acre farms laid out by the Patroon's surveyors. Stephen Van Rensselaer III had advertised and promised them a situation whereby they could occupy the land rent free for seven years.

In the more settled areas of the county, there was now time to pay attention to public improvements. Better communications were being established with other localities as public roads were opened in several directions and stage line franchises were granted to enterprising individuals, though traffic by water was still the easiest and most common. White-sailed Dutch sloops plied the Hudson River to the fast growing commercial center at its mouth. Their holds were filled with the farm and forest produce of Albany County.

Dutch Settlers of Albany County

In the seventeenth century, the people of Holland lived in a prosperous country of toleration and culture. The Dutch enjoyed the material things of life and had a love of substantial furnishings and pictures. They adorned their homes with ornaments and art works which were both decorative and colorful. Pictures were readily available in Holland and some were brought to the New World and hung in the homes of the early settlers of Albany County.

By the first half of the eighteenth century, there were artists in this area who began to paint the portraits of wealthy landowners and prosperous merchants. Although we do not know the names of all of these artists, the portraits they painted survive in our local collections. These early artists or "limners" of the Hudson Valley had artistic talent, but probably lacked much formal training. The portraits they painted are based on European style and tradition. Although the artists appear to be largely self-taught, they painted fairly realistic faces and put an emphasis on bold outline and pattern. They added distinctively American touches, such as a lady holding a single rose in her hand, or a child with a pet bird resting on an extended finger.

Many of the limners copied the poses, costumes and backgrounds from known sources, especially the English mezzotint engraved portraits that were then being introduced into the Colonies. Because the limners had not received any large amount of professional instruction, many of the portraits seem stiff and flat, with not enough shadows to give roundness to the sitter, and the anatomy is often not drawn properly. The formalized backgrounds of some of the paintings, with their use of columns, drapery and curved balustrades, remind us of a Baroque composition. Many of the portraits, some of them three-quarter or full length studies, are large, colorful likenesses.

Some Hudson Valley limners inscribed their portraits with the words *Aetatis Suae*, or various abbreviations thereof, which means "of that age", and denoted the age of the sitter and the date at the time the portrait was painted. Each limner had his own individual technique and is identified by us as the Schuyler or the Gansevoort limner, *etcetera*. These are the family names of the sitters, to indicate paintings which are attributed to a particular artist whose actual name has not been discovered yet. However, the limners, so named, painted portraits of others, as well as those in a particular family. Gerardus (1695-1746) and Evert (1677-1727) Duyckinck, Pieter Vanderlyn (1687-1778) and John Watson (1685-1768) are known painters of Albany County citizens of the colonial period. Pieter Vanderlyn, for example, came to New York from Curacao about 1718 and in 1730 was listed as a firemaster in Albany.

Anthony Van Schaick *(1720), oil on canvas, 46½" x 38½", inscribed lower left "Etats. Suae: 38 Years 1720", attributed to the Schuyler limner. Courtesy, Albany Institute of History and Art.*

Anthony Van Schaick was a son of Anthony, and grandson of Goosen Gerritse Van Schaick, who came early to Rensselaerswyck and was a brewer at that place. Anthony lived in the Van Schaick house on Van Schaick Island and was commissioned lieutenant and then captain of militia by Governor Hunter in 1717 and 1725. He also was named by the Colonial Legislature to act with Captain Jacobus Van Schoonhoven in laying out highways in the Halfmoon Patent, north of Albany. He married, in 1712, Anna Cuyler, daughter of Johannes Cuyler and Elsje Ten Broeck.

The artist probably painted what his sitter was wearing. Anthony Van Schaick's shirt and stock are white, but his coat is russet in color, which blends with the blue and russet background of the portrait. The gloved hand is seen in many American versions of this pose by this limner, and its prototype was probably taken from the English mezzotint of *The Right Honorable Charles Montagu*, a mezzotint by John Smith, 1693, after Kneller. There are similarities to that print in the placement of the hands, the pose of the body and its proportions in relation to the background and the canvas area.

Abraham Wendell (1715-1753) was the son of Evert and Engeltje Wendell, who inherited, upon his father's death in 1750, the family house and lands and a saw and grist mill on the Beaver Kill at the southern end of the city of Albany.

In the Wendell painting, the pose and costume may be inspired by a mezzotint, and the hand thrust into the waistcoat adds an air of self-assurance to the pose. However, the background landscape of the portrait shows the sitter's own mill and lands. This portrait is important because it depicts what is probably one of the earliest actual American landscapes. The mill was located in the ravine near the present day swimming pool complex in Lincoln Park. The mill's location is indicated on the 1794 DeWitt Map of Albany.

Abraham Wendell (1737), oil on canvas, 35¾" x 29½", attributed to the Wendell limner. Courtesy, Albany Institute of History and Art, gift of Governor and Mrs. Averell Harriman and three anonymous donors.

Lavinia Van Vechten (ca. 1720), oil on canvas, 39" x 33¾", attributed to the Schuyler limner. Courtesy, Brooklyn Museum.

It is believed that Lavinia Van Vechten was a young woman of Albany. Her portrait has many similarities in pose, hand placement and gown style to others painted by the Schuyler limner. In the portrait, the sitter wears a dark red dress with cream colored collar and cuffs. The fruit that she holds in her hand is pink and cream colored, as are the two flowers. She has brown hair and eyes. The background is quite dark; the sky behind the figure is brownish-blue above, changing to brownish-red below.

The linear and chaste style of the Gansevoort limner is apparent in the portrait of Adam Winne, baptized 1725, son of Dirkje Van Nes and Daniel Winne of Bethlehem. Adam married Geritje Schermerhorn in or before 1748. While colonial children were painted as little men and women, there is a childish charm and winsomeness to the portraits of children.

The Gansevoort limner is probably Pieter Vanderlyn who was active between 1730 and 1745, painting portraits in the Albany-Kingston area. The Hudson River is portrayed in the background of the picture. Unlike most other limners, the Gansevoort limner tended to portray subjects in their own poses and setting, not borrowing from the mezzotints.

Adam Winne (1730), oil on ticking, 32" x 26½", inscribed lower right "AW 1730", attributed to the Gansevoort limner, probably Pieter Vanderlyn. Courtesy, Henry Francis duPont Winterthur Museum.

Ariaantje Coeymans (1672-1743), a Dutch woman of many legends, was born in Albany and died in her Coeymans stone house. Her father, Barent Coeymans, came from Holland in 1639. At age 14, he became an apprentice or "junghen" under Pieter Cornelise, in the grist mill owned by the Patroon Van Rensselaer at North Albany. In 1673, Barent Coeymans was granted the Coeymans Patent, on land which he had purchased from the Indians. Over a period of years, there was a boundary dispute over this land between Coeymans and the proprietors of the Van Rensselaer Manor. This was finally settled on **August 26, 1714**, when Queen Anne confirmed the **patent to Andries Coeymans, heir of Barent.**

Ariaantje received her land as a grant from her oldest brother, Andries, who divided up the property with her and two other brothers after the death of their father in 1710. She and her brother, Samuel, built the stone house that is still standing at the mouth of Coeymans Creek, and at 51 years of age she married David Ver Planck, age 28.

For nearly a century, Ariaantje's almost life size portrait hung in the stone house. It is believed to have been painted about 1717. She wears a dress of steel gray, trimmed with black and brown. The red rose in her hand complements the shades of pink in the background scene. The source of the Italianate background is from the mezzotint of Lady Bucknell, ca. 1686, after Sir Godfrey Kneller, the most important English portrait artist of his time.

Ariaantje Coeymans *(Mrs. David Ver Planck) (ca. 1717), oil on canvas, 79⅝" x 47½", attributed to the Schuyler limner. Courtesy, Albany Institute of History and Art.*

Caesar *(1849), pencil on paper, 6½" x 4", G. W. Woodward.
Courtesy, Bethlehem Historical Association.*

In the spring of 1736, Elizabeth Salisbury, daughter of Francis Salisbury of Catskill, was married to Rensselaer Nicoll, nephew of the Fourth Patroon, Kiliaen Van Rensselaer. Among the wedding gifts were several negro slaves, a present from the bride's father.

In 1737, a boy was born to two of these slaves, named Caesar. The master's eldest son, Francis Nicoll, was born in 1738 and over the years Caesar became that young man's playmate, valued companion and willing follower. When Rensselaer Nicoll, at about 60 years of age, reached the condition the 18th century called "second childhood", Caesar was about 30 years old and it became his duty to watch after the master. On August 5, 1776, slipping away from Caesar, Rensselaer Nicoll fell into the nearby creek and drowned in 18 inches of water. Francis Nicoll then became the master of the estate, and Caesar drove the horses and in other ways looked after the family's comfort. When Francis Nicoll died, Caesar was 80 years old and he claimed and was granted *the privilege of age*, ending his years of labor and spending his remaining years sitting often in a large chair near the fireplace.

Caesar was inherited by William Nicoll Sill, grandson of Francis Nicoll, and was given a room on the ground floor of Bethlehem House, the family estate at Cedar Hill, where he lived for over thirty years. When Caesar passed away in 1852, at the age of 115, he was buried in the Nicoll-Sill graveyard beside the old homestead where he had been born, having seen six generations of his master's family and five of his own.

The pencil sketch was made in 1849 by G. W. Woodward of New York while Caesar was sitting in his chair at Bethlehem House, asleep. In 1851 he was persuaded to have his daguerreotype taken and the picture conveys an impression of remarkable vitality and physical vigor. It was published in the New York Genealogical and Biographical Society Record for January 1925.

The head of the Schuyler family in America, Philip Pieterse Schuyler, came from Holland before 1667 and settled at Beverwyck (Albany). In 1672, he purchased property, known as de Vlachte (The Flatts), located four miles north of the settlement, on the road to Saratoga.

That the Schuylers soon became members of the landed aristocracy of colonial Albany County is very apparent when one considers the trading and real estate interests of Johannes Schuyler, son of Philip Pieterse Schuyler and his wife Margarita Van Slichtenhorst, the daughter of the first director of the Colony of Rensselaerswyck. Johannes was born at Rensselaerswyck in 1668, died, 1747, and was buried in the Dutch Church at Albany. He was the tenth mayor of the City of Albany, and the grandfather of General Philip J. Schuyler.

Johannes' father had died when the boy was five years of age. While yet a young man, Johannes became interested in public affairs and was active, with his brother Colonel Philip Schuyler, in the control of the city during the period of Leisler's Rebellion. After the burning of Schenectady in 1690, he went with Governor Winthrop's army to pursue the French and Indians to Canada, and until 1693 he was active in colonial conflicts on the frontier. In 1694, he married, at Albany, Elizabeth Staats Wendell, widow of Captain Johannes Wendell. She was the daughter of Dr. Abraham Staats, who came to Beverwyck as a surgeon in 1642, along with Domine Megapolensis, pastor of the First Reformed Dutch Church. Their four children were: Philip, Johannes Jr., Margarita and Catalyntje.

Johannes Schuyler served as mayor of Albany from 1703-1706. Because of his great influence with the Indian tribes, he served as Indian Commissioner from 1705-1723. Johannes was a fur trader dealing mainly in beaver skins and he also owned a fleet of sloops for providing river transporation. His land transactions included several large purchases east of Schenectady, east of the Hudson and in the Schoharie Valley. In 1702, he purchased from Abraham Wendell a portion of the Saratoga Patent, which included the falls near Schuylerville, where he erected mills and built a residence. This house was inherited by his son, Johannes Jr., who, in turn, passed it to his child, General Philip J. Schuyler. This Schuylerville house was burned by the British during the Revolutionary War, and later reconstructed by General Schuyler. The Albany residence of Johannes Schuyler stood at the southeast corner of State and Pearl Streets and it was in this house that his grandson, General Philip J. Schuyler, was born in 1733.

The double ¾ length portrait of the Schuylers has a center vertical seam and it originally may have been two companion portraits that were later pieced together. The pose of Johannes Schuyler has similarities to the Sir Godfrey Kneller *Self-Portrait* of 1720 and the William Shirley mezzotint by James McArdell after Thomas Hudson. The painting is mentioned in the will of Johannes Schuyler, drawn in 1741-42.

Captain and Mrs. Johannes Schuyler *(ca. 1715-1735), oil on canvas, 71" x 54", attributed to the Van Rensselaer limner, probably John Watson. Courtesy, New-York Historical Society, New York City.*

The Dutch sought purpose and direction for their lives in the Bible and their scripture history paintings depict Biblical events that had a special social or religious meaning for them. They found many parallels between Biblical stories and their own historical struggles against outside domination. They valued these scripture paintings for their decorative effect in the home, as well as for their reflections of religious morality. Scripture paintings, products of the same period and the same artists as the portraits, were copied from, or inspired by, engravings in Dutch Bibles that the early families who settled in the Albany County region brought with them or sent for from Europe. These, along with the portraits, are the first and last surviving Dutch art in America. Persons in the scripture paintings are dressed in the clothing of the 17th and 18th centuries and were placed before a contemporary Dutch or Italian background, rather than reflecting the costumes and backgrounds contemporaneous with Biblical times. Many Dutch artists of the 17th century who illustrated the Bibles had studied in Italy and their pictures reflected the influence of earlier Italian Renaissance painters.

In *The Marriage at Cana*, the painter took for his inspiration the engraving in a Bible printed in Holland in 1702, one copy of which belonged to the Van Rensselaer family. The poses, forms of the vases, the four niches and other details are drawn directly from the engraving.

Christ on the Road to Emmaus was a painting which, at least in the 19th century, was used in summer to conceal a fireplace opening at Cherry Hill, the home of Philip Van Rensselaer built in 1787, just south of the City of Albany. The source for this painting can also be traced back to the 1702 Bible illustration. The placement of the figures, road, trees, river, town and bridge is the same as for those in the original engraving. Four other versions of this painting also survive.

Another type of early art that survives are the *hatchments*, family armorial escutcheons painted on board or canvas, which were used as symbols of mourning and owned by families of means and importance. At the time of family funerals they were carried in procession and hung on the family house or in the church. The Ten Broeck hatchment is painted in oil on canvas and the predominant colors are red and silver white, on a black background.

The Marriage at Cana *(early 18th century), oil on canvas, 39¼" x 31¼", probably Albany County. Courtesy, Albany Institute of History and Art.*

Christ on the Road to Emmaus *(early 18th century), oil on canvas, 34½" x 32½", probably Albany County. Courtesy, Albany Institute of History and Art.*

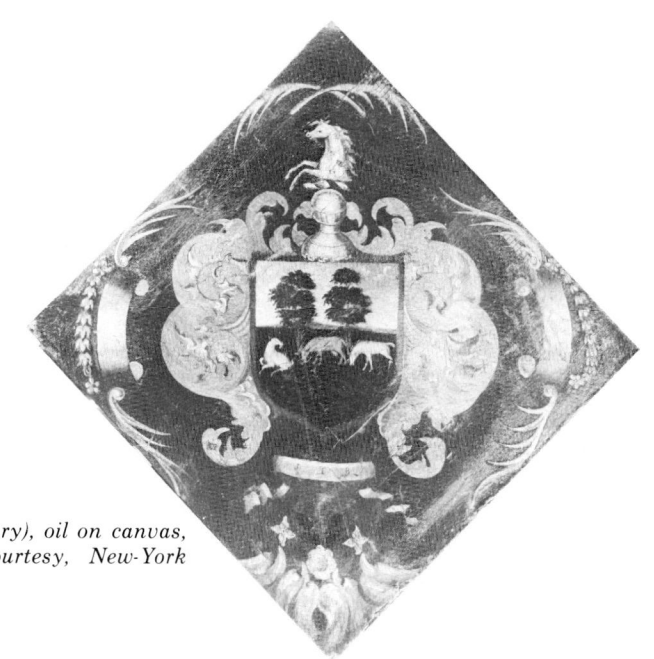

Ten Broeck Hatchment (early 18th century), oil on canvas, 23¼" x 22¼", unidentified artist. Courtesy, New-York Historical Society, New York City.

Dutch Colonial Architecture

A few of the Dutch colonial houses of Albany County still are to be found standing along the river shore and the banks of the principal streams. These houses were inspired by the medieval Gothic tradition of building that prevailed in northern Europe from at least the 13th century. The first people to step ashore in New Netherland were interested in providing themselves with shelter as quickly as possible and had only the time and means to build rude dwellings. As soon as they were able, however, they began to reproduce the one and two room houses they had known in the Old World, not out of sentiment, but because it was the only style of building that they knew. They were adapted, of course, to the climate, resources and topography of the New World. Since the history of Albany County has been one of progress and development, with an eye to the future more than the past, we find no buildings still in existence that date earlier than circa 1720.

The town houses of the Dutch at Fort Orange (Albany) were reminiscent of houses still standing in Holland today. They were a distinctive, regional style not found in any other of the American colonies. These homes, small, closely built residences of wood or brick, or a combination of both, had a steep roof of single pitch, with the straight-sided gable end facing the street, as seen in the Dutch town house that was later known as the *Pemberton* building. Originally the home of Jacob Garret Lansing (1681-1767), this house stood on the northeast corner of Columbia and North Pearl Streets when it was built in 1710 and came into the possession of the Pembertons in 1818. It was demolished in 1886 to make way for the new buildings of the Albany Business College. These town houses often did double duty as a house and shop and second story doorways in some of them provided a convenient way to hoist heavy goods into a second floor garret area.

Pemberton House (1710), Columbia and North Pearl Streets, Albany.

Teunis Corneliese Slingerland was born in 1617 and emigrated from Holland to New Netherland in 1650, settling for a time in Beverwyck (Albany). By the 1680's he had settled along the Onesquethaw Creek on land which he purchased from the Indians. Portions of the original purchase have remained in the family down to the present time. It is believed that a grandson, another Teunis Slingerland, built this brick and fieldstone house on the property in 1762. Although such a late date is attributed to this house, in its style it is typical of Dutch colonial architecture in the city of Albany built in the earlier part of the 18th century, and it bears many similarities to the Lansing-Pemberton house.

Slingerland House (1762), Feura Bush.

The red clay hearth tile before the fireplace in the front room of the Slingerland house is an intriguing example of 18th century folk art. The *running deer*, initials *TSL* and *Cornelis slengerlant* was probably impressed into the wet clay from a furniture brand. These furniture brands were fairly common in the 18th century and were a design which was made up by the owner.

Hearth Tile, Slingerland House (1762), Feura Bush.

This was an age of wrought iron hardware, and the massive hinges and wrought iron beam anchors found on these early houses are very decorative. The beam anchors tied the heavy framing to the masonry walls. Those on the Pemberton and Slingerland houses are in the *fleur-de-lis* pattern, which was common to Albany County Dutch architecture. Wrought iron hinges and latches also secured the wooden shutters, which could be closed over small casement or sash windows.

Proud Dutchmen sometimes had their initials or the date of erection of a house affixed to the brick walls in wrought iron, as in the 1710 date on the Pemberton building and the initials of Tobias C. Ten Eyck (1723-1791), on his home in the Pictuay section of Selkirk. Tobias was the son of a noted Albany silversmith, Coenradt Ten Eyck (1678-1753), and he built his house in 1762 on the banks of the Onesquethaw Creek, on land received from his uncle, Samuel Coeymans. The bricks used in building the house were made from clay taken from the banks of the creek and were fired on the property. Records list brickmakers in Rensselaerswyck at a very early date. Tiles first were used on roofs, but soon were replaced by the more easily made wooden shingles.

Wrought Iron initials (ca. 1760), Tobias Ten Eyck house, Selkirk.

The raised pine paneling of the fireplace wall in a room of the Appel-Slingerland house at Feura Bush is typical of 18th century fireplace wall treatment. This paneling also encloses a floor-to-ceiling cupboard. Old traditions state that the right side of the same fireplace wall encompassed a paneled, built-in Dutch alcove-type bed. This house is believed to have been built ca. 1717.

Paneling (early 18th century), Appel-Slingerland house, Feura Bush.

Ariaantje Coeymans house (ca. 1720), Coeymans.

In the rural areas, the houses were of wood, brick, or more usually of the readily available limestone and the main axis of the house was almost always broadside to the roadway. Usually the house consisted of two or occasionally three rooms in a row, each containing an outer door. The house of Ariaantje Coeymans at Coeymans was built ca. 1720 and is an elaborate example of a country house of the period. Ariaantje, her brother Samuel (1670-1754) and his wife Katrina Van Schaick (b. 1690), resided in this house. Katrina was a sister to Anthony Van Schaick of Cohoes. Another sister, Gerritje Van Schaick, (b. 1687) married the silversmith, Coenradt Ten Eyck and was the mother of Tobias C. Ten Eyck of Pictuay (Selkirk).

Staircase (ca. 1720), Ariaantje Coeymans house, Coeymans.

Originally the Coeymans house was a two story house with a gable roof, but in 1792 changes were made and a new gambrel roof was put on, enlarging the third story. The house was built with a central stair hall, having two rooms on each side. The cherry staircase with its heavy, turned balusters is original to the house and has kinship with the heavy Jacobean woodwork of Europe. The stairs rise from the first floor to the attic, with Dutch tiles placed along the wall as a mopboard in the halls.

The entrance doors on Dutch houses were divided in the middle so that it was possible to keep the bottom section closed while having the top section open to let in light and air, as in the Daniel Frans Winne house, built before the Revolution, near the Vlaamanskill Creek at Selkirk. This type of door was used in houses in Albany County until the early years of the 19th century.

Dutch doorway (mid-18th century), Frans Winne house, Elm Avenue, Selkirk.

Chimneys were built inside the walls in the gable end of Dutch houses and served a hooded, jambless free-hung fireplace with no sides. Illustrating this is the reproduction Dutch fireplace exhibited in the Dutch Room at the Albany Institute of History and Art. These fireplaces were a derivative of northern European types and the fire was built directly on a wide brick or stone hearth, under the large flue. A hood was dropped about 18" from the ceiling over the hearth to channel the smoke into the chimney flue. The hood was enframed by a heavy molding with a wide top edge that formed a mantel shelf, upon which would be displayed the family's earthenware or pewter. Sometimes a wooden boxed-in alcove-type bed was built along a wall.

Dutch room with fireplace (reproduction), Albany Institute of History and Art.

Whitbeck house (1741), Aquetuck.

"Cooksackie, 12 Feb. 1787: After breakfast set out with our company for Indian Fields. After several dillemmas, about ye road, and getting out of it several times, we arrived at Peter Whitbeck's in Aughticoke (Aquetuck). Found Mr. Whitbeck living in an elegant house, built of hewn limestone, house 1½ storys high with two rooms and a hall on the floor. This was situated on a pleasant spot near a creek and surrounded by an intervale. Mr. and Mrs. Whitbeck were gone to Albany to purchase wedding clothes for their daughter, who is about to marry Captain Van Bergen's son. (Mayke Whitbeck (1769-1825) married Peter Van Bergen). We were entertained by Mrs. Ten Eyck, another daughter, who was married very young and has a child, tho' almost a child herself." (Catherine Whitbeck (1770-1845) married in 1785 John Ten Eyck (1771-1834), son of Tobias of Pictuay (Selkirk).

This quotation from *Memoirs of an Emigrant — The Journal of Alexander Coventry* refers to the house of Andries Whitbeck (1707-1765), built at Aquetuck in 1741. The house was typical of the early Dutch country houses of the area, but over the years it has been considerably altered by additions and the raising of a third story.

The Dutch barn on the Vanderzee-Slingerland farmlands on County Route #301 in the Town of Coeymans is typical of barns built in this style from the late 1600's until about 1810 in Albany County. These barns were patterned after the tithe barns of medieval Europe. They still are to be found in scattered locations in the Mohawk and Hudson valleys.

Slingerland Barn (18th century), Feura Bush.

The outbuildings of the country were usually built of limestone and this early one on the homestead of Johannes Appel, son-in-law of Teunis Slingerland, on the Onesquethaw Creek Road, is by tradition called a *slave house*, possibly providing living quarters for the family servants. It contains one room with a fireplace in the end wall and also could have served as a kitchen or wash house. The Dutch settlers of the area did have negro slaves, although not in large numbers, and they were employed chiefly as household servants and farm hands.

Stone outbuilding (early 18th century), Feura Bush.

Bethlehem house (1736), Cedar Hill, Courtesy, Mendel, Mesick, Cohen, Waite architects.

In 1719, Kiliaen Van Rensselaer, the Fourth Patroon, willed a tract of land (1300 acres) at the south side of Bethlehem Creek (Vlaamanskill Creek at Cedar Hill), to Rensselaer Nicoll (1706-1776), the son of his sister, Anna. There had been settlement here at a very early date and undoubtedly the reason was the power available at the falls of the creek. Van Rensselaer records show that a saw mill was erected here soon after the one at the Normanskill was built in 1632.

In 1735-36, about the time of Rensselaer Nicoll's marriage to Elizabeth Salisbury of Catskill, he built the north part of Bethlehem House for his dwelling place. From construction evidence, it is apparent that the house originally was built as a two story brick house with a gambrel roofline. This style of house and roof became popular around Albany in the 1760's. This house, however, would be one of the earliest houses in Albany County to have a gambrel roof. The original "mousetoothing" or tumbled brick pattern of the south wall gambrel can be seen in the attic section of the southern extension, and from this we know that the brick was not painted originally.

At Rensselaer Nicoll's death, the estate passed to his son, Francis, who had married his second cousin, Margaret Van Rensselaer of Claverack. Francis Nicoll (1738-1817) served as a state senator in 1797-98. It was he who added the southern extension in 1795, which was nearly identical in style on the outside to the original structure. In 1812, a kitchen wing was added on the west rear, and in 1820 there was another addition to the rear. These successive enlargements and additions have camouflaged the original Dutch colonial house.

The earthy, decorative quality of Dutch colonial houses is due to the exposure of their construction features. The house framing structure, small-paned windows, heavy batten-type shutters secured with wrought iron hinges, the knee-braced heavy ceiling beams, white plastered walls and thick wooden doors give a medieval feeling to the architecture. Being conservative in nature, the Dutch settlers clung to their 17th century building style until well into the 18th century.

A Brighter Destiny

The Reformation spread across Europe, and many of the people of Holland had adopted Calvinistic Protestantism as their national religion by the 16th century. The directors of the Dutch West India Company gave their sanction to the Reformed Dutch Church and this became the first established religion in New Netherland. Even today, most Hudson Valley towns and cities sustain a Reformed Church, which had its beginnings in colonial times.

The first church service in New Netherland was conducted by Bastian Jansz Krol at Fort Orange in 1624. He was not an ordained minister, but a *Krankenbesoecker* (comforter-of-the-sick), who was permitted to conduct services by reading the Liturgy and Dutch sermons. The first congregation in Albany was founded in 1642 with Domine Johannes Megapolensis (1601-1670) serving as pastor. He was the first Protestant missionary to the Indians and a number of them united with his church at Albany. He preceded by several years John Eliot in New England as an Indian missionary.

The two communion beakers of the First Reformed Church at Albany are among the oldest colonial silver in this country. The beaker was a communion vessel of cylindrical form with curved lips and succeeded the medieval chalice. The beaker on the left was made in Holland in 1660 by an unknown maker, and sent over for use in the original wooden church, built in 1656. The communion beaker on the right was made by one of the first silversmiths in New Amsterdam, Ahasuerus Hendricks in 1678. The beakers are decorated with a double intersecting strap band filled with flowers. Three oval panels are engraved with the figures of Faith, Hope and Charity. Large clusters of fruit are suspended from the band, surrounded with engraved cherub figures. Three birds on branches are engraved at the bottom of the body.

Communion beakers (17th century), 7⅛" x 3⅜". Courtesy, First Church in Albany (Reformed).

The oldest known weathervane in America is the weathercock of brass made in Holland and sent over in 1656 for the First Church. The bullet hole is said to have been made by an Indian discharging his fowling piece.

The Reformed Dutch Church was still in its infancy in New Netherland when the English conquest came in 1664. There were probably not more than 8000 people in New Netherland at the time and not all were members of the Dutch Church. Almost all immigration from the Netherlands ceased after 1664. The church no longer had financial support from the Dutch West India Company. For many years, it stubbornly clung to the Dutch language for church services. For its future growth, the Church would rely upon the descendents of the early settlers, or what converts it might secure.

Evert Duyckinck (b. ca. 1620 - d. after 1700) came to New Netherland before 1640 and was listed as a *glazier* in early records. He executed the window sash with painted coats of arms for placement in the first Dutch church in Albany in 1656. His Van Rensselaer window and the window of Rutger Jacobsen are two that survive in museum collections. These windows are the earliest form of Dutch colonial art still in existence.

With the coming of the English, the Church of England was established. Today it is called the Episcopal Church. The garrison at the fort and the few English families in Albany occasionally were visited by the chaplain of the fort at New York in the early years. By 1708, the Reverend Thomas Barclay was serving as chaplain at the fort in Albany. He organized a parish and in 1714 the Crown granted a patent for an English church, constructed in the center of Jonker Street (State Street). This denomination remained largely a church of rich merchants, officials and large landholders. It suffered during the Revolutionary War from its close connection with the Crown and the reluctance of some of its members to back the Colonial war effort. The communion plate owned by St. Peter's Episcopal Church is one of two sets sent over to America by Queen Anne in 1711-12. One set is still used by the Mohawk Indians in Canada and the other is at St. Peter's.

The Presbyterians were as strong as the Anglicans during the colonial period in Albany County because of the immigration of Scottish and Ulster Irish settlers. There was a Lutheran congregation in Albany as early as 1656. In fact, the First Lutheran Church in Albany is the oldest Lutheran congregation in this country. These congregations were the infant beginnings of religious life in Albany County.

Weathervane (1656). Courtesy, First Church in Albany (Reformed).

English Georgian Influences

During the 1760's there was a great spurt in the building of substantial and spacious dwellings within Albany County. The English culture was taking precedence over the Dutch and this was reflected in domestic architecture. These houses also reflected a new degree of wealth and sophistication that had been attained by the descendents of the first settlers, now that the seemingly interminable wars with French Canada finally were over.

What was later known as the Georgian style of architecture first became popular in England in the late 17th and early 18th centuries, and it incorporated dignity, formality and regularity. Many of its principles were based on the works of Andrea Palladio (1518-1580), who built handsome Renaissance villas for wealthy Italians in the 16th century. His design ideas, incorporating certain classical features, resulted from his study of the ancient monuments of Rome and the writings of the early builders, Vitruvius and Alberti. In 1570 he published a four-volume work on architecture that was translated into many languages and became a source of great influence in the western world. In England, Palladio's ideas were tranlated into handsome buildings by the famous architects Inigo Jones, Christopher Wren and others, who adapted classical design to contemporary need.

With English ideas beginning to prevail in the Hudson Valley, it was only natural that the populace should abandon the northern European Gothic type of architecture and adopt the newer styles brought about by changed social, political and cultural values. English builders published their own illustrated books of Georgian designs and these were widely read and copied during the first half of the eighteenth century. Such books found their way into the hands of the carpenters in America, who adapted the designs to local needs and climatic conditions. These 18th century colonial houses marked a breakaway from the purely functional form of house building to a new emphasis on features of formal symmetry and careful proportions. They had an improved floor plan that permitted better circulation, more comfort and privacy.

The Van Schaick house at Van Schaick Island, Cohoes, built ca. 1755 by Anthony Van Schaick, grandson of Goosen Gerritse Van Schaick, is situated on a section of the *Halfmoon Patent*, originally granted to Goosen Gerritse and Philip Pieterse Schuyler in 1664. Since varying dates are given for the erection of the Van Schaick house, it is probable that there was a dwelling house on Van Schaick Island at this site in very early years.

The steep medieval roofline of earlier times was modified in the Georgian period to a roof of lesser pitch, or replaced with a hipped or gambrel roof, flattened at its peak, as in the Van Schaick house. The gambrel roof was not Dutch at all, as many have assumed, but was shown in English building books in the 18th century and was used in New England houses of the 17th and 18th centuries.

These modified Georgian type houses were usually one room deep with a center hall and entrance door, and one and a half stories in height. On the interior, the open fireplace of the Dutch was replaced with the English style, which had jambs reaching from floor to ceiling. A new treatment appeared in the fireplace wall, which was paneled with beveled wood and the opening surrounded with heavy molding, although a mantel shelf was not yet usual.

Van Schaick house (ca. 1755), Cohoes.

The one-and-a-half story house began to be replaced by a house of two stories. The Schuyler Mansion is the most elaborate example of the Georgian style of architecture still in existence in Albany County. Its construction was begun in 1761, four years before the building of the Van Rensselaer Manor House. In his diary of 1785, Alexander Coventry wrote, "Schuyler has a large and elegant mansion at the south end [of the town]. It is, however, exceeded by one at the north end, belonging to Mr. Van Rensselaer, called here Patroon, and Lord of the Manor. He married a daughter of General Schuyler."[3]

The bricks for the Schuyler house were made by Lucas Hooghkerk, one of a family of local masons and brick makers, who had a brick yard on Gallows Hill. The master mason was William Waldron. There is a balanced look to the facade of the house, with square-headed windows placed in ordered rows, framing a center entrance door. Other houses of the same period often had a three-part Palladian window placed over the front door, and the entrance doorway was framed with moldings or pilasters and topped with a pediment. The hexagonal entrance vestibule was added ca. 1818 by a later owner of the house, John Bryan, and has remained virtually unchanged since its construction. It is possible that the vestibule may have been designed by Philip Hooker, but there is no actual proof that this is so. However, there is a watercolor of the house, complete with vestibule, that was prepared by Hooker in 1818, as part of an evaluation of the property. The roof balustrade, in a Chinese motif, may have been added during Schuyler's lifetime, or perhaps in the early part of the 19th century. The Schuyler Mansion has a four-room plan with center hall extending from front to rear, so that it was not necessary to go through one room to reach another. In 1762, while Schuyler was in London, he ordered hardware, glass, carpets, draperies and wallpaper for the house. The interior was finished under his supervision after his return.

Schuyler Mansion (1761), Broad and Catherine Streets, Albany. Courtesy, New York State Office of Parks and Recreation, Division for Historic Preservation.

In the Georgian house, stairways gained more elegance as a decorative feature and stair balusters became more slender. In the Schuyler Mansion, the three balusters on each stair are turned in three different spiral patterns and the handrail is supported by a turned newel post. It is probable that John Gaborial, the master carpenter, came from Boston to work on the house. It is known that he ordered the stairway to be shipped to Albany from that city. The archway dividing the hall may originally have been completely open, with the leaded fanlight possibly installed in 1818 when the vestibule was added. This has similarities to the work of Philip Hooker, but there is no documentary evidence to support its installation by Hooker.

In 1780, Elizabeth Schuyler married Alexander Hamilton in this formal drawing room of the Schuyler Mansion. In the later part of the 18th century, increased importance was placed on ornamenting the fireplace wall, and some chimneypieces received a broken scroll pediment and carved ornamentation in the more elaborate houses. The four marble facings and hearths used for some of the fireplaces in the Mansion did not arrive in Albany until after July 1767, when they were shipped from Philadelphia by David Chambers, a marble mason. The use of Philadelphia marble for this purpose was popular into the 19th century. The elaborately carved cornice, wainscoting, crystal chandelier and fine furniture bespeak the wealth and importance of the owners.

Stairway, Schuyler Mansion (1761), Broad and Catherine Streets, Albany. Courtesy, New York State Department of Commerce.

Drawing Room, Schuyler Mansion (1761), Broad and Catherine Streets, Albany. Courtesy, New York State Department of Commerce.

Cherry Hill, 1787, So. Pearl Street, Albany. Courtesy The New York State Department of Commerce.

Among the last of the Georgian-type expressions of architecture to be constructed in the Albany area was the home of Philip Van Rensselaer, known as Cherry Hill. The house was built in 1787 and is located on South Pearl Street in Albany. Originally the Cherry Hill farm encompassed 900 acres of land and was situated in the Town of Bethlehem. This area was annexed to the city in the later 1800's.

The Cherry Hill family descended from Hendrick Van Rensselaer (1667-1740), a brother of the third Patroon, who owned much acreage at Greenbush and Claverack. Hendrick's grandson, Philip Van Rensselaer (1747-1798), acquired the Bethlehem tract about the time of his marriage to Maria Sanders (1749-1830) of Albany in 1768. On this land he built the Cherry Hill house. Philip Van Rensselaer was a commission merchant in Albany and he also maintained a residence in Albany on North Pearl Street. At the time it was constructed, Cherry Hill served as their country farm home.

One of Philip's twelve children, Arriet (1775-1840), married her cousin, General Solomon Van Rensselaer. They resided at Cherry Hill for over 60 years and were some of the better known tenants of the house. Solomon Van Rensselaer was especially noted for his services with the army during the War of 1812.

The Cherry Hill house is a full two-story frame structure, with large attic and a fieldstone cellar containing kitchen and storage rooms. The house was covered with a wood-shingled gambrel roof and originally contained 20 rooms. The plan is typical of Georgian design with a passageway from front to rear and two flanking rooms on either side on the lower and upper floors. Captain Isaac Packard, an Albany carpenter, was the builder of the house. He attained a degree of elegance within the house by the use of varied mouldings and symmetrical balance, as well as the use of color on the walls and woodwork. Early records indicate that many of the rooms at Cherry Hill were wallpapered, a luxury at that time. Over the years there have been additions and room changes which have given the house a total of 34 rooms and 10 fireplaces.

Originally the road which ran in front of Cherry Hill was named the Bethlehem Turnpike; it is now South Pearl Street. The road to the north of the house (now First Avenue) originally went up the hill westward to Whitehall, the home of the Gansevoorts.

The Gerrit Van Zandt (1730-1806) house, called by him "Oriskatach", was built ca. 1755 on the Onesquethaw Creek Road above Feura Bush. It served as a farm home of the period and perhaps as a fortified outpost. Tradition states that prisoners of the French and Indian Wars were kept in this house and the basement windows have iron bars such as one finds in a fortress. The attic is one large barracks-type room.

Van Zandt was a colorful character but only meager records of his many business dealings in Albany County have filtered down to the present time. His wife was Hester Winne, who died in 1813 at the age of 81 years. Van Zandt's grandfather lived in Albany as early as 1713 and Gerrit Van Zandt not only maintained this country farm on the Onesquethaw, but he had a home in Albany as well. He dabbled in politics and in 1752 was constable for the First Ward in Albany and in 1773 was alderman for that ward. Bills of sale record that he was active in the slave trade and he was also a merchant in Albany and an agent for New York City wholesalers. He held the position as a deputy commissary for stores for the British forces in North America from 1767-1775, in which he was responsible for supplying the troops moving through the Albany area with necessary food, mainly pork and flour. Perhaps some of this was raised on his farm along the Onesquethaw. His position made him suspect at the outbreak of hostilities against the Mother Country, and he was called before the *Commission for Detecting and Defeating Conspiracies*, but he seems to have satisfied that body as to his allegiance. Van Zandt was involved in land speculation as early as 1766 and continued in that until the time of his death.

Gerrit Van Zandt house (ca. 1755), Feura Bush.

In rural areas of the county, a more modest type of house was constructed, of wood or brick, and quite often of stone masonry, adapting English architectural styles to simpler American materials and needs.

The Coeymans-Bronck house at Coeymans, along the banks of the Hannacroix (Crowing Rooster) Creek, was built ca. 1770 by Charlotta Amelia Coeymans (b. 1727) and her husband, Jan Jonas Bronck (b. 1724). The door on the west is at ground level, but the main entrance to the house is on the east, facing the Hudson River. The main entrance has a raised *stoep* (porch) which was originally flanked with two wooden benches and there is a fine 18th century entrance door in the Dutch style, although the plan of the house is Georgian.

Time spans are assigned to an architectural style for definitive purposes, but certain particulars of every style in house building persisted beyond their time period, especially in rural areas. Elements of the Dutch culture were carried over into buildings of the Georgian period. An overlapping of styles occurs whenever the many aspects of architectural development are considered.

Coeymans-Bronck house (ca. 1770), Coeymans.

Aspirations Toward Elegance

By the 1750's, immigrant artists from Europe had brought a more refined form of painting to America, and one that exhibited a stylish realism and reflected increasing technical skill.

Affluent Americans wanted portraits that would look suitable and decorative in their larger and more elaborate Georgian houses and drawing rooms. They wanted portraits that would continue the trend toward an air of elegance and reserve that was depicted in the painting style of the English Court. These portraits did not necessarily emphasize the personality of the subject, but they had an atmosphere of charm and grace and were decorative. They did make more use of light and shadow, give more grace to the body, finer modeling of the features, more flowing motion to the garments, and use more detail than the earlier colonial limner had painted in his portraits.

Thomas McIlworth, an itinerant painter from Scotland, turned up in the region of Schenectady and Albany ca. 1762-1769. He painted in a bold, effective style and his colors were harmonious and pleasing. He achieved a likeness that was able to suggest the subject's age reasonably well, although he often used an identically repeated formula in the poses and costume treatment. Nevertheless, his portraits, and others of the period, reflect the elegance that the people who posed for the portraits had attained, and they were valuable historical documents of the mid-18th century upper class.

The portrait would be the most prolific form of art until near the second quarter of the 19th century. There was as yet no great impulse among artists to turn to other types of painting, such as landscape and still life. Perhaps the wilderness was still too near, too much an element to be conquered, to make it attractive as an art object.

The portrait of Catherine Van Rensselaer Schuyler (1734-1803), painted by Thomas McIlworth, dates from her wedding or early married life. Catherine was the daughter of John Van Rensselaer of Fort Crailo and his wife Engeltje Livingston Van Rensselaer, and thus she was a direct descendant of Kiliaen Van Rensselaer, the First Patroon. Mrs. Schuyler's portrait is copied from a mezzotint of Elizabeth, Duchess of Hamilton, ca. 1752, by Richard Houston after a painting by Francis Cotes. Despite some improvement in technique in these later pictures, there is still a certain hardness to the portrait and the sitter is still depicted in a rather rigid pose.

Catherine Schuyler (ca. 1762-1767), oil on canvas, 30" x 25", Thomas McIlworth. Courtesy, New-York Historical Society, New York City.

General Philip Schuyler (1792), oil on wood, 9.6 x 7.9 cm., John Trumbull. Courtesy, Yale University Art Gallery.

Johannes Schuyler Jr., the nineteenth mayor of Albany, was the father of General Philip Schuyler (1733-1804). Johannes had been active in the mercantile business and furnished supplies to the forts at Oswego. He also invested heavily in land at Saratoga, Little Falls, and the east side of the Hudson, above the Saratoga Patent. He married Cornelia Van Cortlandt and died at the age of 41 when Philip was but a young child. Attesting to the family's influence was the fact that five of Philip Schuyler's relatives served as mayors of Albany.

When Philip was 15, he was sent to the Huguenot School at New Rochelle, where he excelled in the French language and mathematics. At 18 he returned to Albany and set out on a trading expedition to the Mohawk wilderness. In 1755, he was married to Catherine Van Rensselaer of Fort Crailo and was also marching against the French at Crown Point. His real talent lay in handling supplies, and by 1756 he was a member of the quarter-master staff of General John Bradstreet, carrying provisions to Oswego and forming a lifelong friendship with Bradstreet, despite a great difference in age.

In 1760, General Bradstreet was called by the English government to account for his handling of public funds and supplies. Since he was needed at the war frontier, he requested Philip Schuyler to represent him in London in settling his accounts with the War Office. Schuyler satisfactorily attended to General Bradstreet's affairs and then toured England, studying especially the canal systems, which he envisioned as someday being introduced into his own country. By this time, too, Philip and Catherine Schuyler had selected land for a new home about a half mile south of the city of Albany. While Philip was away in England, General Bradstreet had his power of attorney and assisted Mrs. Schuyler in planning for the new home. When Schuyler returned in 1762 from London, the house was nearing completion. During this time, and indeed throughout his life, Philip Schuyler was a landowner and land speculator, merchant, financier and gentleman farmer, all as a means of livelihood and building his estate.

The years following were a period of turmoil within the colonies concerning the policies of Great Britain with respect to her American settlements. Schuyler maintained a moderate position, but finally affairs forced him to join the rebellion against British rule. In 1775, he was one of four Major Generals commissioned by the Continental Congress and he was given charge of the Northern Division of the Army. Volumes have been written about Schuyler's participation in the Revolutionary War. Let it suffice to say that he was a whole-hearted patriot, struggling against great odds and the carelessness and jealousies of those who were to supply him with troops and supplies. When Burgoyne invaded New York, it was Schuyler who planned and executed the tactics that delayed the British force. It was Schuyler's urgent pleas that brought an increasing force of militiamen to augment his small army. encamped on Van Schaick's Island, preceding the battle at Saratoga. The New England faction, challenging the Dutch leadership and desiring the appointment of General Horatio Gates in place of Schuyler, spread many rumors about him. On the eve of the Battle of Saratoga, the Continental Congress relieved Schuyler of his command. Later, his honor was vindicated completely.

With the Revolution behind them, the leaders of Albany County allied themselves into various political factions to gain control of civil affairs and weld a new State constitution. Philip Schuyler was an active political leader in the Federalist Party, and in 1789 became a member of the U.S. Senate. He was an advocate, with his beloved son-in-law, Alexander Hamilton, of a strong Federal Union with centralized powers. He continued advocating a canal system and was a director of the Western Inland Lock Navigation Co., incorporated in 1792, to plan a navigable waterway for the state.

Mrs. Schuyler died in 1803. Ailing and elderly, Schuyler further was distraught by the tragic death of Hamilton in 1804, and he passed away that same year at the Mansion.

The portrait of General Philip John Schuyler was painted in miniature by John Trumbull at Philadelphia, in 1792. Schuyler is painted in his uniform as a Major General in the Continental Army.

Patriots of the New Country

Leonard Gansevoort (1751-1810) was practicing law in Albany at the time of the Revolutionary War and served in the Provincial Congress in 1775. He was chairman of a Committee of that Congress that had an intelligence network to detect conspiracies and bring Tories all over the Province under control. After the War, he built up the family mercantile business, and, turning to politics, was elected to the U.S. Congress as a Federalist in 1788. The Federalist Party was composed largely of the landed gentry and wealthy merchants. Leonard Gansevoort, as well as other patricians of Albany County, attained their positions within it by virtue of their political activity and business prominence.

In 1793 a fire swept along the north side of State Street, between Pearl and Broadway. Leonard Gansevoort lost his house and store in this disaster and consequently moved his family to another of their properties, known as *Whitehall*, located near the present intersection of Delaware Avenue and Whitehall Road. General Bradstreet, Amherst's supply officer in the French and Indian Wars, had purchased Whitehall in the 1760's and it was used by the British Army then as their Albany headquarters. After the Revolution, having been confiscated as Tory property, it was bought by John Schuyler, son of General Philip Schuyler. Leonard Gansevoort purchased it from Schuyler in 1789.

In Bradstreet's time, the house had a reputation for luxury and great hospitality. Leonard Gansevoort kept up the tradition of conviviality by adding two large wings, making it into an H-shaped dwelling suitable for holding large social functions. At this time, he was the first judge of Albany County and later served as a State Senator.

Gansevoort's daughter, Magdalena, who had married Jacob Ten Eyck in 1795, received the Whitehall mansion when Leonard died in 1810. From this inheritance, the house descended through the Ten Eyck family until it burned in 1883.

Mourning art was much in vogue in America in the first part of the 19th century. Instruction in the art was probably given to young ladies in the academies and seminaries by teachers of art and needlework. The mourning pictures were made as a tribute to a departed loved one. They were sometimes painted on silk or other material and many were embroidered. The two young women pictured in the Gansevoort mourning picture are undoubtedly the daughters of Leonard Gansevoort — Magdalena, the wife of Jacob TenEyck, and Catherine, who married Teunis Van Vechten in 1813. Typical elements of mourning are depicted, such as the urn, plinth and willow tree. The mansion and barn are personal expressions added by the individual maker.

Whitehall mourning picture (ca. 1810), 11" x 7½", Courtesy, Indian Ladder Farms, Inc., Voorheesville.

Frederick Krownsky (1714-1777), son of a Polish nobleman who had fled to Wurtemburg, Germany, immigrated to New York in 1754 with his wife Elizabeth, and his son, George Frederick, leaving a son, Philip, behind in Germany.

Landing at Rhinebeck after a journey up the Hudson River by sloop, they found little available land near Albany and decided to continue on toward Schoharie, where others of their countrymen were settled. Arriving at the site of their future homestead under the Helderberg escarpment, they decided they had traveled far enough, and so secured a lease of several hundred acres of land from the Lord of the Manor of Rensselaerswyck. For 13 years they labored to improve their farm and in 1767, their son Frederick took as a bride Anna Weber, who had also come to America from Wurtemburg. That same year, too, their son Philip came over from Germany with his wife and two children, to make the family circle complete. He secured a farm adjoining that of his father, on Gardner Road, Town of Guilderland.

Philip had been in America only eight years when the Revolutionary War broke out. He enlisted, becoming a Sergeant in the company of Captain Jacob Van Aernam, whose farm adjoined his own. His brother, Frederick 2nd, served as an Ensign in the same company. This Third Regiment, Albany County Militia, was in active service from 1779 to 1781.

At the time of the Battle of Saratoga, it is recorded that General Abraham Ten Broeck came to the Helderberg region and requested the tenants to send as much of their provisions as they could to feed the troops at the battle site. The Crounses, as well as others, complied, and when the war was over, their efforts were not forgotten. The Patroon called Frederick Crounse 2nd to the Manor House and there offered him the opportunity of buying his farm, which he held under lease. For 295 pounds Crounse purchased his 226 acres of land from Stephen Van Rensselaer.

Frederick Crounse 2nd, born 1747, was also an officer of the Town of Guilderland and of St. James Lutheran Church, (now demolished) the first between Albany and Schoharie. The church was located halfway between the villages of Altamont and Guilderland Center. Frederick Crounse died in 1828 and is buried in a little plot behind the Crounse homestead on the Voorheesville-Altamont Road. His gravestone, carved with the mourning symbol of the weeping willow tree, is illustrative of the distinctive stone sculpture found in early cemeteries as a result of the neo-classical revival of the late 18th century. This sentimentalized cinerary urn and/or willow motif form of gravestone carving, beginning ca. 1790, replaced the earlier winged death's head and winged cherub carvings and it was popular until ca. 1840. These early carved stones are an important form of American folk art.

Gravestone of Frederick Crounse (1828), Altamont. Courtesy, Arthur Gregg.

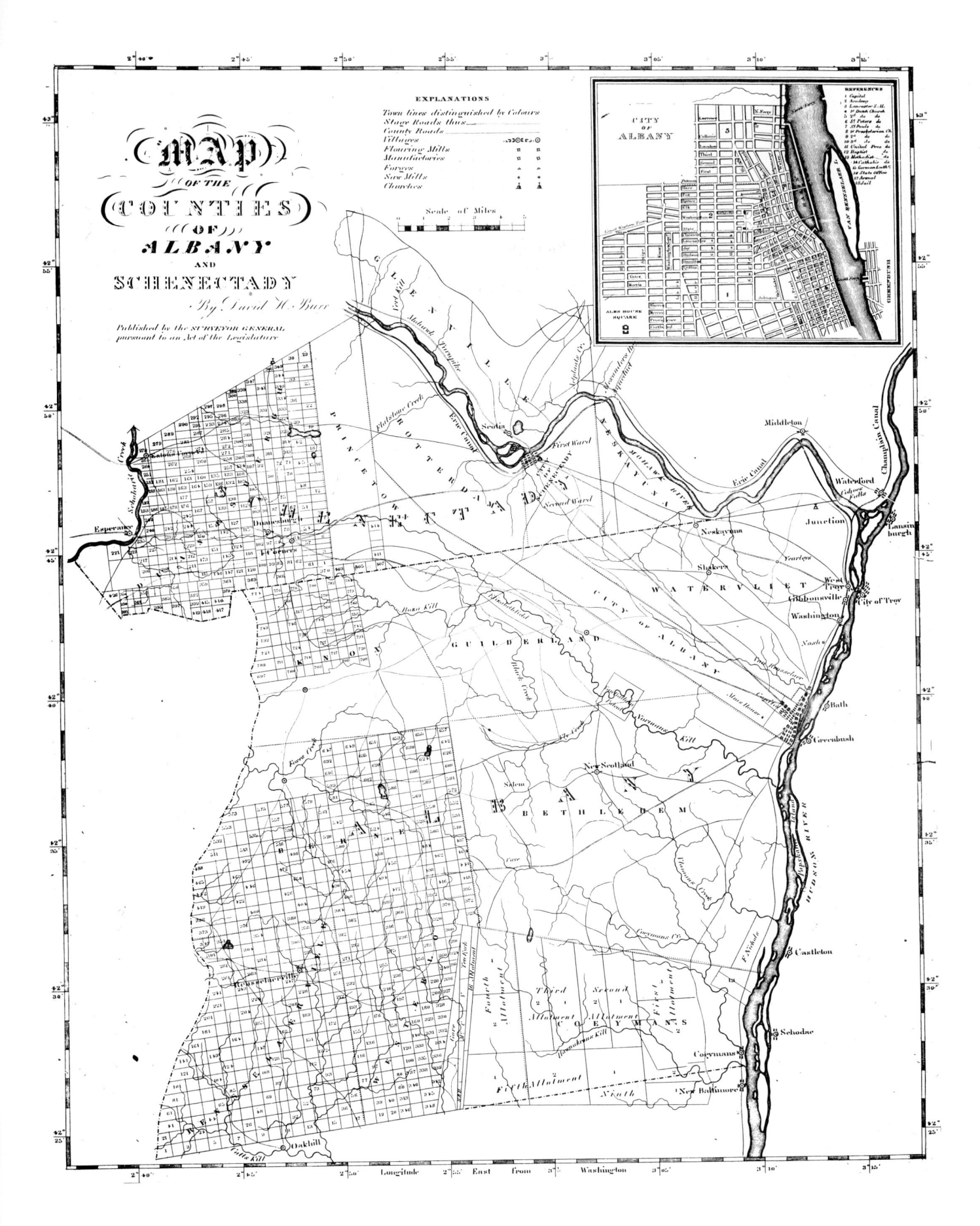

Map of Albany County by David H. Burr (1829), engraved by Rawdon, Clark and Co. of Albany. Courtesy, New York State Library.

CHAPTER II

A New Dawn for Albany County
1785 - ca. 1830

The anguish of a people had ended in triumph. A new republic was being established in a spirit that rarely had been present in the world since the days of ancient Greece and Rome. A fresh wave of opportunity was stirring in Albany County and a free people were turning their attention toward a new day. After the Revolution, a long period of peace settled upon Albany County. There was progress in all directions, with a large growth in population, as hundreds of New Englanders made their way westward to settle in the area. Travel to and from Albany was facilitated by new turnpikes and Albany became the turnpike and staging center of the state. Eight new turnpikes radiated out from the city and these greatly increased its importance as a place of trade and commerce and made it the principal gateway to the west.

The year 1790 found Albany County with three incorporated towns — Albany, Rensselaerville and Watervliet. By 1800, the increase in population and a need for a more manageable local government brought into being the towns of Berne, Bethlehem and Coeymans. Before another fifty years elapsed, the remaining six would be erected. There was a beginning of settlement in all the isolated areas of the county. Forests were being cleared; there was much more cultivation of the land and building of mills in new places. A desire for a higher level of education brought about the building of school houses. The church still exerted a powerful influence in people's lives and was the center of community life. The Dutch descendents of the earliest settlers were active in the political, agricultural and mercantile forces of the county. Along with them, a new host of enterprising speculators and traders from the New England area immediately after the Revolution brought new vigor that helped make Albany County into a commercial center. By the year 1813, there were 300 mercantile firms listed in Albany, selling a variety of goods.

This northern county that had been an outpost of civilization on the edge of a wilderness when the war ended, now found that its doors were opened wide to the movement of a great tide. People in search of riches and land in abundance were starting to rush to the great open frontier beyond the hills of Albany County. Migrating colonists journeying west began to appear on the city streets and at the river ferry crossings. In 1795, upwards of 500 oxcarts a day made their way up State Street hill. In one three day period in February of that year, 1200 sleighs passed westward through Albany toward the Genesee Valley. The cold northern New York winter did not deter the eager pioneers. The dirt cart tracks were miserable roads and travel over the frozen ground was preferable to the mud and sandy ruts of the path in summer.

In 1797 a significant honor came to Albany County. The city of Albany was selected to be the capital of New York State. It had a strategic location and had played a significant role in State history in peace and war during colonial days. Nevertheless, the honor had been hard fought and won by a very close vote. The public square behind Fort Frederick on the hill was designated in 1804 as the site to be set aside for the first Capitol.

This remarkable era was not to continue however, for war clouds again began gathering on the horizon. Great Britain gave the Americans much cause for complaint with her high-handed measures against our vessels on the open seas. The War of 1812 saw a suspension of all American commerce, and advancement within Albany County was greatly retarded during this period. The city and county of Albany again became a rendezvous of the military, with all the attendant numbers of troops and supplies passing through on their way westward toward the frontier at Lake Ontario.

Greater prominence, however, was soon to be brought to Albany County by three developments that came in quick succession. The era of transportation was about to begin — the topography of the State was exceptionally favorable for its development. Traffic on the Hudson River would never be the same slow pace

Early wagon road, opened in 1828 as a shortcut to the Towns of Berne and Knox. It ascended the Helderberg escarpment from the Voorheesville-Altamont road. The road site is still visible in John Boyd Thatcher Park. Courtesy, Arthur Gregg.

again after 1807. In September of that year, Robert Fulton's North River steamboat (later called *Clermont*) completed the first successful steamboat voyage from New York to Albany. By 1840, there were over 100 steamboats on the Hudson, making it one of the world's busiest rivers.

Influential men in the county could see very clearly the importance of improved transportation facilities. The rapidly increasing population in the western portion of the State would be sending back down river bulk produce of their own area. In turn, they would need manufactured goods and merchandise in trade. There was thus a lively interest in canal building by far-seeing individuals. With the expansion in the west, the times were right and canals were advocated by newspapers and political circles. In 1817, after much involved political struggle, the Legislature passed a bill authorizing the construction of a great canal connecting Lake Erie with the Hudson River and Lake Champlain. By 1825, *Clinton's Ditch*, the Erie Canal, linked Albany County to the Great Lakes and the city's population doubled within a few years. The *Albany Basin* was constructed and soon sheltered a thousand canal boats and 50 vessels of a larger class. This boat basin was constructed at the termination of the Erie and Champlain canals at the city of Albany to improve wharfage facilities for storage and trans-shipment of goods. All of this volume of traffic brought prosperity to Albany County because it became a warehouse and freight shipment point for commerce. The produce brought on the canal was sent down the Hudson in giant tows of up to 50-100 barges lashed together, towed behind a single steamboat. Hundreds of Albany County residents had jobs working on the boats or at the dock areas. There were numerous docks and wharves servicing the country people along the Hudson at the county's eastern edge. A busy traffic in passengers and freight and farm produce was carried on at Van Wie's dock, Winnie's dock at Cedar Hill, at Coeymans Landing, and at West Troy (Watervliet).

Even with the success of steamboating and the building of the canals, there was yet, in the developing stage, a third enterprise that would be so superior in efficiency to rival forms of transportation that it would relegate these to the background. Before the canals had reached their zenith, one of the first passenger steam locomotives in the country made a run from Albany to Schenectady at 15 miles per hour, in 1831. This was faster than any boat could travel. Promoters were fired with new dreams of prosperity and progress. The railroad was being seen as a competitor to the flourishing commerce of the canal. The element of time was quickly equated with profit and loss by the men of business. Rail lines were chartered by the

Erie Canal Entrance Into the Hudson at Albany *(1824)*, after a drawing by James Eights, engraved by Rawdon, Clark and Co. of Albany. In Amos Eaton's "A Geological Survey of the District Adjoining the Erie Canal in the State of New York", 1824. Courtesy, New-York Historical Society, New York City.

Legislature throughout various sections of the State, many of them having a terminus in Albany, once again giving the city a pivotal trade position.

All of this was the stage setting for the titans of industry and commerce that were to shape the future development of Albany County. The county was becoming what it is best known for today: a place of passage, a place of warehousing and distribution, and a financial center of upstate New York. The future had begun long ago in the history of the Indians and the Dutch fur traders. The theme would be repeated again and again as trade and commerce reached fuller development in the years ahead.

THORP & SPRAGUE,
(FORMERLY POWELL & THORP.)
NORTHERN & WESTERN,

Stage & Canal Packet Boat Office,

No. 365, North Market-street,
NEAR THE MANSION HOUSES & POST OFFICE.

COACHES leave this office every morning and afternoon for Schenectady, Little Falls, Utica, Sacket's Harbor, Auburn, Geneva, Canandaigua, Rochester, Lewiston, Buffalo and Niagara—through to Buffalo in three days.

For CHERRY VALLEY, Madison, Manlius, Syracuse, Elbridge, Montazuma, Lyons, Palmyra and Pittsford, to Rochester, every day.

For COOPERSTOWN, every Monday, Wednesday and Friday.

For SCHENECTADY, every morning and afternoon to meet the Packet Boats for Utica and Rochester. Extras with regular relays of Horses, will be furnished on short notice on any of the above routes.

THORP & SPRAGUE, *Proprietors.*
Albany, June, 1825.

Advertising poster for Thorp and Sprague stagecoach line and canal boats (1825). Courtesy, Town of Colonie.

In the Federal Style

Although the Revolution had brought political freedom, allegiance to British social and cultural values was discarded slowly by the Americans. Yet they did not cease looking to England for their architectural styles.

In the mid-18th century archeological discoveries and excavations at Pompeii in Italy had caught the world's attention. The delicacy and grace of the designs of classical antiquity influenced Robert and James Adam of England to publish a set of architectural manuals. These manuals soon found their way to America where they were widely used and copied, and influenced Federal period architecture.

The Federal style — corresponding to the years in which the new federal government and its institutions became established — had some basis in the classicism of the Georgian period. However, the style was more refined and delicate in treatment. The farmhouse built by Frederick Britt (1745-1811), ca. 1801, on Route #32, Delmar, has many elements of this classicism. The entranceway has pairs of engaged columns on either side of the door, which support a pediment containing a semi-circular window. A three-part Palladian window is above the center door. Having served in an Ulster County regiment during the Revolutionary War, Frederick Britt later came to settle in the Bethlehem area and married Helena Burhans, daughter of early settlers in Bethlehem.

Britt-Luke house (1801), Delmar.

The elaborate chimney piece of the Georgian era disappeared, as fireplace walls became plastered rather than paneled. A delicate and refined Adam-style mantelpiece of graceful proportions developed sometimes in a simple "country" style, as the mantel in the Britt-Luke house, beautifully executed with carved fan ornamentation on the colonnettes. Urns, garlands, swags, rosettes, occasionally an eagle, and the radiating fan and ellipse were used in the elements of design. In New York, in particular, these last two shapes were extravagantly used to decorate wooden surfaces.

Mantelpiece, Britt-Luke house (1801), Delmar.

A variety of gracefully curved stairways added ornamentation to the hallways. Twisted balusters disappeared after the Revolution and were replaced with simple square or round ones. The simple newel post and balusters in the stairway of the Frederick Crounse homestead, built in 1803 on the Altamont Road in the Town of Guilderland, illustrate the clean lines of the Federal period in country architecture. The hall doorways still have the heavy wrought iron hinges and thumb latches familiar in the colonial period.

Stairway, Crounse house (1803), Altamont. Courtesy, Arthur Gregg.

The little house that Ephraim Russ (1745-1853) built for Gurdon Conkling in Rensselaerville in 1825 has an air of elegance and an atmosphere of airiness and delicacy that was totally lacking in the more solid medieval styles of earlier times. The low pitched roof, smooth facade and windows in arched openings are all hallmarks of the Federal style, although the arrangement of doors and windows within the pedimented portico is unusual.

Most Federal houses in Albany County had two stories, a center hall, two or four rooms to a floor, and were built of brick or wood. Their shape generally was that of a rectangular box of slender proportions, with delicate moldings and detailing light in scale. In the Federal period, too, variations began to be made in floor plans to increase convenience, and rooms serving a particular function were added, such as: pantries, libraries, dressing rooms and clothes closets. Room design was altered to include oval or octagonal shapes for reception and ballrooms, and ceilings became higher and windows larger, adding to the feeling of spaciousness.

Conkling house (1825), Rensselaerville.

Arched doorways with semi-circular leaded fan lights replaced the square colonial openings, as in the entrance door at the Albany Academy, built in 1815 by Philip Hooker.

Entrance door, Albany Academy (1815), by Philip Hooker. Academy Park, Albany.

Philip Hooker (1766-1836) was one of the earliest native professional architects in Albany County and at one time most of the important buildings of Albany were of his design. In 1772, Hooker moved from Massachusetts to Albany with his parents and as a young man worked with his father, Samuel Hooker, who was a carpenter-builder. Samuel Hooker left Albany to settle at Utica about 1803, but Philip stayed on in Albany. Philip Hooker seems to have received the inspiration for his buildings from the classic revival style of Charles Bulfinch (1783-1841), Asher Benjamin (1771-1845) and John McComb (1763-1853), and he adapted their designs to his early Albany structures. He apparently studied English architectural manuals, but his work was less sophisticated, less monumental in scale and definitely American in flavor.

The city of Albany increased rapidly in population from 1790 to 1830. The citizens wanted buildings in the new classical style, as opposed to the traditional native Dutch, for their new homes and business enterprises. Philip Hooker was able to supply their needs. In 1797, Hooker received his first commission as an architect with his design for the Reformed Dutch Church in Albany. The classical motif is apparent in the pedimented projecting pavilion of the front entrance with its monumental columns and the arched window openings suggestive of the Roman idiom as popularized by Thomas Jefferson (1743-1826). In the later 19th century, the front entrance portico was changed substantially from the one shown in the drawing. Hooker designed in Albany seven religious structures, two and perhaps three of the banks of his day, both of the principal academies, the City Hall of 1829, the State Capitol of 1804-09, the Pearl Street Theater and three municipal markets.

He did not stay only upon the local scene, but constructed Hyde Hall near Cooperstown for the Clarke family, the chapel at Hamilton College and churches and a bank for Utica. He also drew plans for private residences in Albany and Utica, although none of his Albany houses survive. Not only was he busy with architectural pursuits, but also he was active in political circles as well, serving as assessor and alderman, City Superintendent from 1821-1827 and City Surveyor from 1819-1832.

The doorway of the Reynolds House at 99 Columbia Street, Albany, may have been done by Hooker about 1830. This doorway was removed when the house was torn down in 1929 and is preserved in the collections of the Albany Institute of History and Art. The shell design above the door is classical in inspiration, as are the pillars on either side of the entrance door. The doorway is built on a curve and the fanlight arches upward and forward to form a half-dome.

Reynolds house doorway (probably by Philip Hooker, ca. 1830), Albany. Courtesy, Albany Institute of History and Art.

In his style, Hooker tended to use the architectural modes of earlier times, echoing Palladio and the Italian Renaissance manner. His buildings had a pleasing quality, although they sometimes lacked unity and variety of treatment. In his later work there were signs of a different style emerging. He modified the Renaissance lines of his buildings to those of the Greek Revival, although he never attempted to reproduce the temple-like facade. Two examples that exemplified this trend were the Albany City Hall of 1829 and Hyde Hall in Otsego County, with an enlargement of the house in 1833.

Johannes Fisher came from Long Island to Berne in the late 1700's and settled on a farm along the banks of the Fox Creek. Called by tradition a "slave house", but more probably a kitchen and wash house, this brick outbuilding is located on the former Fisher farm. The interior of the building is one large room with a fireplace in the end wall with a bake oven and a large iron pot set into a brick retainer which has a place beneath it for a fire. This large pot could have been used to heat water for laundry purposes as it seems much too large to have been used for cooking. There is a half-round window over the entrance door and on the rear of the building is this reconstructed bee-hive oven that was used for baking. The opening for this oven is on the interior fireplace wall. As far as is known, there is but one other bee-hive oven (so named because of its shape), still in existence in Albany County and that one is in ruins.

Johannes Fisher had eight slaves in 1800; perhaps some of them slept in the loft of the brick building. The Town of Berne was organized and its first officers elected at a meeting held in the farmhouse. Sometime after 1800, a larger Federal style addition was attached to the early sloped roof dwelling, and the house served over the years not only as a home but also as a tavern and a store.

In the early years of the 19th century, our nation was still a frontier country. The graceful style of Federal architecture already was doomed by the desire of people for something more distinctively robust and suggestive in feeling of a republican culture. Before 1830 the stirrings of this new element came to fruition.

First Reformed Dutch Church (1797), by Philip Hooker, North Pearl Street, Albany. Courtesy, First Church in Albany (Reformed).

Brick outbuilding (probably kitchen and wash house) (ca. 1800), Fisher house, Berne.

On August 4, 1797, a fire in the city of Albany destroyed about 95 houses, one of which was the home of Abraham and Elizabeth Ten Broeck, situated near the corner of Columbia and North Market Street (Broadway). After this unfortunate happening, the Ten Broecks decided to move to a less confined area, and built a new home on property they owned to the north of the city, on a rise of land overlooking the Hudson River. In 1798, when the new mansion was complete, it was named "Prospect", because of its favorable position and encompassing view. Since the Ten Broecks were in their sixties when the house was built, they had a relatively short occupancy of their magnificent home. The General died in 1810 and his wife in 1813.

The Ten Broeck Mansion has many progressive stylistic elements for the date of its construction, although alterations and additions have changed some of the character of the original design. While Philip Hooker was the leading designer and builder in Albany during the period that the Ten Broeck Mansion was constructed, we do not have any evidence at present to support the theory that he might have been the designer of the house. The Mansion has the taller, basically rectangular form of Federal residences. The five bays of the main facade express a simple symmetry — facades were usually kept flat with a minimum of projecting detail during this period. A portico was almost universal after 1790, but it was merely an elaboration of the doorway itself. Elliptical or semi-circular fanlights over the doorway were a hallmark of the Federal style, but the Ten Broeck house has a rectangular transom over the east entrance door, which later became the accepted form of the Greek Revival. Fiske Kimball, the architectural historian, has stated that this rectangular transom was one form of early Federal architecture that was found particularly in New York.[4] The west (rear) side of the house has an elliptical headed door with two distinctive stairhall windows — the third floor window being elliptical in shape.

Staircase, Ten Broeck house (1798), Albany.

Ten Broeck house, west side (1798), Albany.

The house has the traditional Georgian plan of four rooms to a floor with the center hall that continued to prevail during the Federal period. The graceful spiral staircase at the rear of the hall, which rises to the third floor, is one of the most progressive and sophisticated features of the Ten Broeck house. Simple balusters and railing express an adherence to slender proportioning. Clever framing is responsible for the graceful upward sweep of the curving stairway, which seems to support itself. The arched niche for the display of a classical bust was another new feature of the house, adding a dimension of elegance.

Mantel, Ten Broeck house (1798), Albany.

Fireplace mantels in Federal houses were usually the decorative focus of the room. Carvings of swags and festoons, sunburst patterns and delicate beadwork composed the mantel, while some type of columnar element flanked the fireplace opening. The mantel in the southwest bedroom of the Ten Broeck Mansion has much carved Adamesque detail in its elaborate central floral decoration and Corinthian columns on either side of the opening.

The Federal design was no longer popular when Theodore Olcott purchased the house in 1848 and renamed it "Arbour Hill". About 1850, many alterations were made by the Olcott family. Some of the fireplace mantels were replaced with plain, stark marble facings of the Greek Revival period. The four Ionic columns that flank the passage between the two north rooms were added at this time, when they were a popular element of decor in sophisticated residences. Also added at this time was the projecting portico of the east entrance. The porch on the west also dates from the Greek period, with its heavy Doric columns and squat proportions, in direct contrast to the height of the main Federal block.

The Olcott family was one of the wealthiest and most prominent in 19th century Albany and the Arbor Hill Mansion was their home for one hundred years. In 1947 it was given to the Albany County Historical Association by the heirs of Robert Olcott, grandson of one of the great financiers of Albany — Thomas Worth Olcott.

East entrance portico, Ten Broeck house (1798), Albany.

It is apparent that Abraham Ten Broeck (1734-1810) would have had a commitment to governmental and civic service because of his family heritage. He was the fifth generation of the family to be settled in New York, Wessel Ten Broeck, the progenitor, having come to New Netherland in 1626 with Pieter Minuit. By 1662 his son, Dirck, was living in Albany and trading in furs. He soon became involved in city government, being Mayor in 1696-1698, as well as being a representative to the Provincial Assembly and the council to the Indians. Dirck's son, Wessel, carried on these same traditions, while continuing a prosperous mercantile trade. Wessel's son Dirck, Abraham's father, also filled a number of these same positions and was mayor of Albany from 1746-1749.

Abraham Ten Broeck was trained to be a merchant, serving in the counting room of his elder brother-in-law, Philip Livingston. In 1763, he married Elizabeth, daughter of Stephen Van Rensselaer 1st, the Fourth Lord of the Manor. Such a union of two important families helped to cement social, political and financial ties, as well as add to the vast landholdings. When the Seventh Patroon, Stephen II, died in 1769, Abraham Ten Broeck was named trustee to supervise the extensive affairs of the Manor for his five-year-old nephew, the eighth Patroon, Stephen Van Rensselaer III.

In 1771, Ten Broeck was elected to the Colonial Assembly as a representative of Rensselaerswyck. He felt, as did many of his contemporaries, that Great Britain was putting into play too many pressures against her American colonies. Becoming involved with various colonial opposition groups, he was appointed in 1775 as a delegate to the Second Continental Congress. That same year he was commissioned a Colonel of the Third Regiment, First Rensselaerswyck Battalion, Albany County Militia. With the coming of active warfare he rapidly advanced to Brigadier General and received his greatest military fame for his leadership at the battles of Saratoga and Bemis Heights. While still serving

Abraham Ten Broeck *(1799), oil on canvas, 50.8 x 40.12 cm., attributed to Ezra Ames. Courtesy, Albany County Historical Association.*

his militia command, he was appointed Mayor of Albany, 1779-1783, and was also a member of the State Senate.

In 1792 he became president of the city's first bank — The Bank of Albany. Always interested in education, he served on boards promoting an academy building, was a trustee of Union College and first president of the Albany Public Library in 1792. One of his great interests was transportation. He was a commissioner of the Western Inland Lock Navigation Co., incorporated in 1792, and was an active promoter of the Albany-Schenectady Turnpike in 1802. From the late colonial period through the beginnings of the new republic, Ten Broeck's record of public service was one of outstanding involvement in the life of Albany County.

His portrait, painted in 1799 when he retired from the bank, represents him in the act of signing bank bills. Letters or documents held in the hand lend a feature of interest in portraits of men, as a personal or professional identification.

Abraham Ten Broeck's grandchildren *(1801), wax portrait, 12¾" x 10½"*, John Rauschner. Courtesy, Albany County Historical Association.

The wax double portrait of Abraham Ten Broeck's grandchildren, Margaret Stuyvesant Ten Broeck (b. 1790) and her brother, Petrus Stuyvesant Ten Broeck (b. 1792), was executed in 1801 by John Christian Rauschner (1760- ca. 1810). Rauschner was born in Germany but had a studio in New York City from 1799 to 1808. Single portraits in wax are much more usual than a double portrait. Rauschner's portraits usually were mounted on glass and the wax was colored all the way through according to medieval tradition. Occasionally he used molds for the figures, pressing the wax into the mold, color by color, and adding finer details afterwards. The Ten Broeck children are portrayed in a woodsy setting. Margaret, age eleven, is seated, wearing a long white dress and has a dog by her side and she is holding a basket of flowers. Petrus, age nine, is holding a bird's nest in his outstretched hands. A great deal of attention has been paid to even the smallest detail in this charming picture.

Margaret and Petrus were the children of Dirck Ten Broeck, Abraham's only son, and his wife Cornelia. The children were born in Albany. Dirck Ten Broeck was a lawyer in New York City and was in his 30's when the Ten Broeck house was built by his parents. He was involved in both city and State politics. Dirck's oldest son, Abraham, spent some years living with his grandparents in Albany.

Samuel Fuller *(early 19th century), oil on canvas, 29½" x 23½", unknown artist. Courtesy, Kenneth Storms.*

While the northern and eastern sections of Albany County were settled mainly by people of Dutch extraction, the southern and southwestern sections were later peopled by emigrants from Connecticut and western Massachusetts, coming in through the valley of the Catskill Creek. Rensselaerville was surveyed in 1786 and a few settlers came in the following year. The Presbyterian Church in Rensselaerville was organized in 1793 and Rev. Samuel Fuller was its first pastor. His life story is indicative of the hardy qualities exhibited by many of the early pioneers.

Born in Connecticut in 1767, Samuel Fuller was graduated from Dartmouth College in 1791. While in college, he heard an Episcopal church service conducted by a travelling minister, which apparently colored his thinking and affected his later life. After graduation he began the study of theology with a pastor in Sheffield, Massachusetts, and in eight months was licensed to preach. He filled pulpits in several towns in the Berkshires and the adjoining portion of eastern New York. In 1792 he married Ruth Pond, of Woodbury, Connecticut.

Interested in settling in New York, in April of 1793 he came alone on horseback, into Rensselaerville, noting in his journal that it was a new settlement with no meeting house. He agreed to preach to the residents for three Sabbaths. In November, he received a call to the ministry in that village, at 100 pounds settlement and 50 pounds annually, on condition that he would remain their pastor for five years. The 100 pounds was paid by deeding him eighty acres of Lot 227 in the Town of Rensselaerville.

In the cold weather of the following February, he went back to Connecticut to bring his family to Rensselaerville - wife Ruth, baby Harriet, and his sister-in-law, Martha Pond. Martha later married Josiah Conkling, a resident of the village. They travelled to Rensselaerville by two sleighs and crossed the Hudson on the ice. The family of four shared a two room log cabin with Mr. Samuel Nichols until April, when they moved to larger quarters.

A Presbyterian church was built in 1796 and the congregation grew from a membership of three persons to 101 members in a few years. In 1799, because money was not available to pay his salary, Samuel Fuller undertook his first missionary journey through western New York. In many new settlements, his preaching was the first that had been heard. In 1804, he went on a second journey, from December until March.

After sixteen years of service to the Presbyterians, the Reverend Mr. Fuller announced that he was resigning to take orders in the Episcopal Church because he could not resolve his doubts about the Presbyterian form of ordination. In 1810, at 43 years of age, Samuel Fuller was ordained and returned to Rensselaerville, where he held the first Episcopal church service. Samuel Fuller passed away in 1842 and his funeral was held in the church that he had founded and where he was the rector for 31 years.

Episcopal Church (1814), Rensselaerville.

In 1814 the Episcopal congregation commissioned a local builder, Ephraim Russ (1784-1853), to build the present church structure at a cost of $2900. Russ's early buildings in Rensselaerville were a refinement of New England architecture in the Federal style. The gallery windows of the simple church give it the appearance of being two stories in height. Ephraim Russ built six documented houses and four churches in Rensselaerville. Several other houses in the area are attributed to him. By 1837, the village of Rensselaerville had four churches and 600 inhabitants and was unusually prosperous and beautiful.

Jenkins house (1812), Rensselaerville.

One of the early settlers of Rensselaerville was Samuel Jenkins. He came in 1788 and built the first mill in the village a year later. While serving in the Legislature, Samuel Jenkins became acquainted with Stephen Van Rensselaer III and formed business relations with him. The Jenkins' homestead was built in 1812 for his son, Jonathan Jenkins, by Ephraim Russ. The quiet dignity of the broad front, with windows balancing the central motif of the pedimented doorway and the Palladian window above the entrance, has similarities to New England architecture.

45

Weathervanes were an important instrument to the farmer in the 18th and 19th centuries and were placed on barns or other farm buildings. These wind indicators aided the farmer in weather forecasting. Weathervanes were also a prominent design feature on the steeples of rural churches in the early years of the 19th century. The vane on the steeple of the Dutch Reformed Church at Berne has a characteristic scroll design common to the period in which the church was built - 1831.

Weathervane (ca. 1831), Berne Reformed Church, Berne.

Weathervane (early 19th century), Albany Academy, Academy Park, Albany. Courtesy, Bureau of Historical Services, City of Albany.

The weathervane which was formerly on the cupola of the Albany Academy building in Academy Park, Albany, replaced an earlier scroll design vane. The weathervane pictured originally was atop the steeple of the Second Presbyterian Church on Chapel Street in Albany. The cornerstone of the church was laid in 1813. The vane was removed to the Albany Academy cupola when the church was transformed into a theater in 1918. The converted church building was torn down in the 1940's. The weathervane is now on the Albany Academy building on Academy Road in Albany. Locally known as the "fish and pumpkin" weathervane, an old tradition states that the symbols, modelled in the round, were emblematic of Massachusetts and Connecticut respectively and were representative of the New Englanders influence on the city of Albany in the late 18th and early 19th centuries.

Mills and Manufacturing

Available water power in the form of swift flowing streams with adequate falls was of great importance in the early settlement of Albany County. Albert Andriessen Bradt commenced milling operations on the Normanskill in 1636 and Barent Pieterse Coeymans came to the Colony in 1639 and worked at a mill in North Albany for the Patroon. Grist and saw milling were the earliest forms of industry in Albany County. The last grist mill in the county to close down operations (Hart's mill at Berne), ground oats, barley and corn for the dairy farmers until 1960. The first grist mills were built to serve the local people and their products were consumed by the people that they served. However, at an early date, wheat and flour were exported from the county, as well as lumber.

The Northeast can lay claim to being the birthplace of the Industrial Revolution in America, which had its beginnings in the early 19th century, primarily because of the available water power for mills. Cottage industry was still an important part of production, but by 1800, spinning and weaving began to move out of the home setting and there was a noticeable shift of many operations to small village shops. The development of industries based on local resources led to stone, brick and wooden mill buildings being built along the banks of the streams. There were cloth and fulling mills, wool carding and dressing mills, straw paper, potato starch and flax processing mills, as well as tanneries and asheries in abundance. One industry attracted another and led to the growth of small hamlets at the mill sites. The picturesque mill with its turning water wheel is long since a thing of the past. The products of past generations have disappeared, too, in Albany County, supplanted by totally different activities. But it was the 19th century that saw locally made products sent beyond the borders of the county to a growing domestic and foreign market.

Advertising Poster, Meneely bell factory, West Troy, N.Y. (1844). Courtesy, New York State Library.

As early as 1811, men had recognized the advantages of the locality around the Cohoes Falls as a suitable site for manufacturing purposes. They formed *The Cohoes Manufacturing Company*, built a dam to supply water power and erected a factory for the manufacture of wood screws. Several other small manufacturing operations were erected nearby. Canvass White, an engineer on the Erie Canal project and a pioneer figure in hydraulic engineering in the United States, recognized the Fall's possibilities and in 1826 formed *The Cohoes Company*, for the utilization of water power in the manufacture of cotton. This also gave the company exclusive use to sell or lease water rights to other businesses. Over the years, numerous feeder canals were constructed to supply water power to the water wheels, and later, for the turbines that drove the machinery in the mills. At one time nine-tenths of the machinery in Cohoes was run by water power obtained from these canals. Although the primary reason for the eventual development of large manufacturing complexes in Cohoes was the available water power, another huge factor in the success of these mills was the proximity of the Erie Canal, which ran through the city, and the ease with which finished goods could be shipped to market.

In the engraving of the City of Cohoes, made in the mid-19th century by an Albany engraving firm, Lewis and Goodwin, the Cohoes Falls and Mohawk River are in the middle of the picture, the first Harmony Mill, erected in 1837, is at the left and the Erie Canal is in the foreground with the feeder canal from the river at the right center.

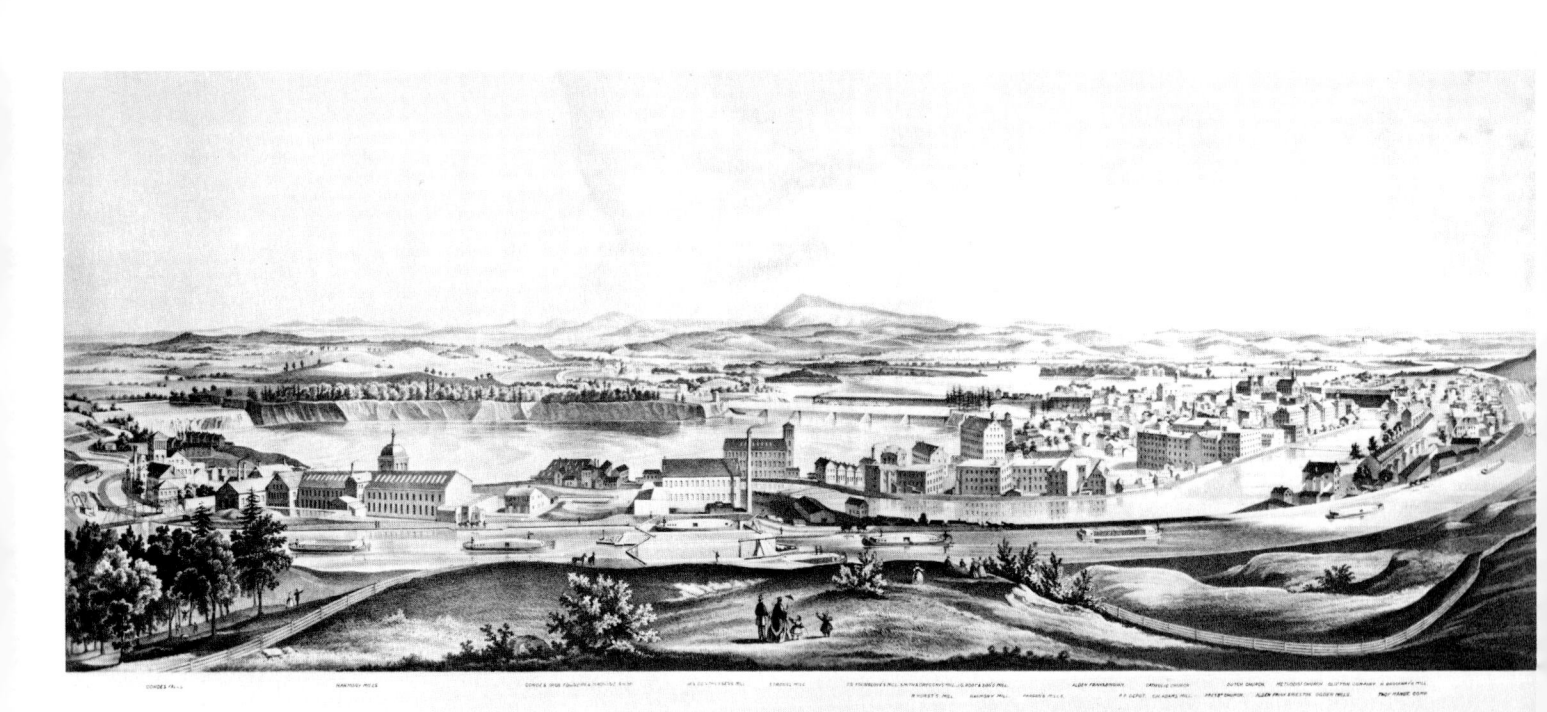

View of Cohoes *(19th century), 37½" x 17½"*, Lewis and Goodwin lithographers. Courtesy, Historical and Cultural Society of Cohoes.

A group of investors incorporated *The Harmony Manufacturing Company* at Cohoes in 1836. With a change in proprietorship in 1850, there was a period of prosperity and growth which led to the construction of many new factory buildings over a period of years. Its extensive facilities and the introduction of more complex machines by mid-century made it the largest and wealthiest cotton manufacturing plant in America, especially after it came under the supervision of Mr. Robert Johnston in 1851. At the height of their production, ca. 1875, the Harmony Mills employed over 5,000 operatives, turning out millions of yards of cloth per year. Harmony Mill No. 3, erected in 1873, was the largest complete cotton mill in the world under one roof. It was part of an industrial complex of eight major mill buildings, plus several secondary structures. The No. 3 mill is five full stories in height, including a usable mansard and dormer attic, plus a full, usable basement. Projecting from the face of each section are six story stair towers that were originally topped with mansard roof caps. The large central pavilion has, at each corner, a highly detailed square tower capped with a mansard roof crowned with decorative ironwork. Most of the molding and detail of the central pavilion is sheet metal. Its handsome French Baroque architecture in granite and brownstone, with mansard roofline and corbel moldings, as well as its significance in the story of the industrial development of this nation, has earned it a place on the National Register.

Harmony Mills #1 and #3 (early and mid-19th century). Courtesy, Cohoes Community Development Agency.

In 1832 Egbert Egberts (1791-1869), born in Coeymans and operating a store in Albany, began experimenting with the application of mechanical power to turn knitting frames, which had formerly been cranked by hand. He moved to Cohoes and with the able mechanic, Timothy Bailey, developed a method of using water power to run knitting machines. These men became the pioneers of knit-goods manufacture in America. They began their venture by knitting hosiery. By 1886, twenty-five knitting mills were in production in Cohoes, turning out hosiery and knitted underwear that represented one-quarter of the knit goods production of the United States.

Mr. Egberts retired from active business in 1852 to enter politics as the Whig candidate for Congress. In 1858, he organized the Bank of Cohoes and became its president, serving in that capacity until he died. He was a wealthy man with great dedication to community improvement. In 1864 he founded an educational facility, the *Egberts Institute*, which was the forerunner of the present Cohoes High School.

Egbert Egberts (ca. 1860), oil on canvas, 41½" x 33½", Charles Loring Elliott. Courtesy, Albany County Historical Association.

By the time of the Civil War the mills in Cohoes had such a great need for labor that over 8000 French-Canadians came to the city to work as mill operatives. The Harmony tenements were built in the simplest style during the years 1866-67. Over $300,000 was spent in erecting these tenements for a thriving mill village of 6000 people. Only employees of the company and their families were allowed to reside in these dwellings.

Mill Tenements (mid-19th century), Cohoes.

Although cotton and knitting mills continued to be the dominant industries in Cohoes in the 19th century, many other manufacturing establishments also were located at Cohoes because of the water and shipping facilities. They produced such goods as iron and steel products, machinery, furniture and paper boxes that were sent out of the county to far away destinations.

In 1825 Daniel Simmons first had established an axe factory in Berne. While working as a blacksmith he had discovered a way to use refined borax as a flux to weld steel cutting edges to iron, and his axes were so superior to others of the time that his business prospered. Eventually, dwindling charcoal resources for fuel and the remote location at Berne made the cost of transportation too great. In 1833, Simmons removed to Cohoes where he could use water power and canal transportation. For over 50 years afterward, edged tools were manufactured in Cohoes as an outgrowth of this business.

By the turn of the century, a depressed market and continuous labor troubles in the form of child labor laws, unionization and numerous labor strikes began to mark the end of the era of prosperity that had come to Cohoes. The economy began to decline as mill operators moved out to other areas of the country in search of more favorable labor conditions. A shift in the American economy would see a drift away from the processing of raw materials and the production of capital goods within Albany County.

In 1806 Nathan Crary invented the wooden pill box, which brought employment and a source of income to the citizens of Knox for almost 100 years. Basswood was used to make the shavings, which formed the sides of the little boxes. At one time there were six factories in Knox producing pill boxes, as well as many homes where the women and girls put the boxes together. The industry supplied boxes to some of the largest pill makers in the country. Eventually, the scarcity of basswood trees and the invention of machinery to turn out tin boxes and glass vials spelled the end of the industry in Albany County.

One of the early industries of the county had its beginnings in Guilderland in 1785 when Jean de Neufville began to manufacture glass on the banks of the Hunger Kill about six miles west of Albany. The venture proved more costly than anticipated and the Legislature was persuaded to make several loans to assist in establishing the glass factory. By 1792, another company had been formed for the manufacture of window glass and glass bottles. After de Neufville died in 1796, several prominent Albany County men, such as Elkanah Watson and Jeremiah Van Rensselaer, carried on the business. The abundance of pine trees in the area as well as the easy availability of potash, a compound made from wood ashes, early provided the necessary means to make glass. However, after a few years of extensive cutting, the trees were cleared away, and it proved too expensive to draw wood from a distance. The factory was closed in 1815.

Nathan Crary *(first quarter of 19th century), water color, 13" x 10", unknown artist. Courtesy, Knox Historical Society.*

The waterproof, imitation beaver hats that were sold on Market Street (Broadway) in Albany were manufactured by Benjamin Knower near his homestead at Knowersville in the Town of Guilderland, present-day Altamont. Benjamin Knower also had a residence in the city of Albany, at 43 Court Street, and later at 132 State Street, since he was a wealthy man of many and varied interests.

Rising to ascendency in the commercial sphere in woolen manufacturing, real estate and water rights, he also was instrumental in the organization of the Albany Mechanics Society in 1793. This Society was in existence from 1793-1824 and comprised of about 150 mechanics and tradesmen and was founded for the purpose of protecting and supporting their brethren, and widows and orphans of the same who were in indigent circumstances. The group also erected school houses and promoted learning to elevate the standard of education within the city.

Benjamin Knower *(ca. 1807), oil on canvas, 30¼" x 24⅜", Ezra Ames. Courtesy, Albany Institute of History and Art.*

In 1811 Knower was elected to the Board of the newly formed Mechanics and Farmers Bank and served as its president from 1817-1834. He was also president of Roy and Company, a mill in West Troy (Watervliet) that wove woolen cloth and shawls. This mill was located on Moordenaer's Kill (Murderer's Creek) in a section of what is today the Albany Rural Cemetery. It was through Benjamin Knower that the Cemetery Association acquired title to the land in 1844. In 1823, he was named a commissioner of the Albany Basin and served on the committee for the celebration of the opening of the Erie Canal. He was State Treasurer from 1821-1824 and directed the celebration of the visit of General Lafayette to Albany in 1825. By this time, too, the period of political control by wealthy aristocrats had lost ground and an upsurge of democratic feeling led to a change in the political scene in New York. The Albany Regency was one faction which exercised control in political circles, and Benjamin Knower was a member of this group, along with his son-in-law, William L. Marcy (who had wed his daughter Cornelia in 1824) and Martin Van Buren of Kinderhook, who became the 8th president of the United States. Knower used his banking and political connections to good advantage in his many speculative enterprises.

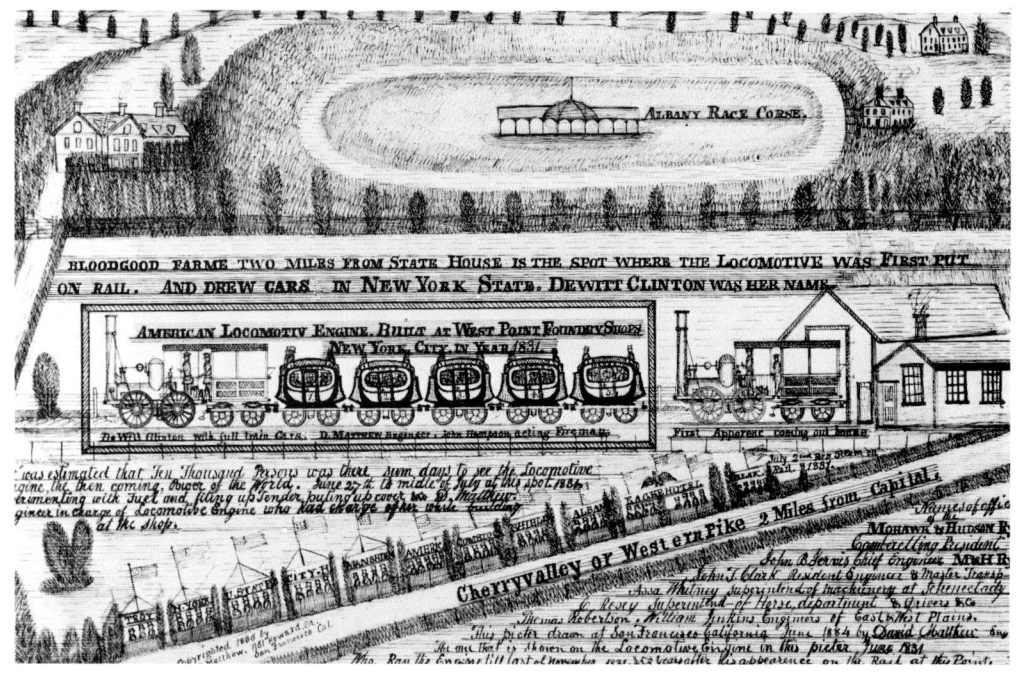

Drawing of locomotive DeWitt Clinton *(1884), pen and ink 17⅜" x 10¾", David Matthew. Courtesy, New-York Historical Society, New York City.*

Goold's Carriage Works grew out of the need for transportation over the network of turnpikes that led to and from Albany during the first part of the 19th century. James Goold (1790-1879) began his factory in 1813, to supply the stage coaches that were soon traveling through the toll gates of the new roads. It was in Goold's factory that the carriages were made for America's early passenger railroad, which ran from Albany to Schenectady, beginning in 1831. The coaches for this train were built to the plan of the road stagecoach and were set on rigid four wheel trucks, at a cost of $310.00 each. As times changed, Goold progressed to the making of carriages and buggies which were well-known for their excellence and style. He also made the *Albany Cutter*, a swell-body sleigh of gracefully curving outline for 2, 4 or 6 passengers. Because of its fluid lines, it was considered one of the most beautiful of American sleighs.

Several other coach and sleigh factories were established and made the city outstanding for the production of these vehicles. The Brewster Carriage Factory, located in Newtonville, also was noted for the manufacture of family and pleasure carriages.

This folk art drawing copyrighted in 1886 by David Matthew, the engineer of the first Mohawk and Hudson Railroad train, gives a good representation of the train and particularly its steam engine, *The DeWitt Clinton*, as well as a great deal of pertinent information. Also depicted is the Albany Race Course. This is probably what was known as the Island Park Racecourse, located about two miles above Albany on the east side of the Troy road, and considered at the time one of the finest and fastest tracks in the country. The original track was built as private property in the 1860's but was incorporated as an association in 1884.

William H. Brown was present on August 9, 1831, to cut the silhouette of one of the early steam passenger trains in America. Work had begun in 1830 on a railroad to cross the 17-mile shortcut from Albany to Schenectady, across the Mohawk-Hudson River bend, a route that had been favored as a portage from earliest time because it bypassed the Cohoes Falls. This silhouette of the first train to run between the two cities, as cut by Brown, was over six feet long and was exhibited widely. David Matthew was the engineer and John Hampson the fireman. The passengers were (from rear of train): 1. Unknown; 2. Lewis Benedict; 3. James Alexander, President of the Commercial Bank; 4. Charles E. Dudley, in 1831 a U.S. Senator whose widow founded the Dudley Observatory in Albany; 5. Jacob Hayes, High Constable of N.Y.; 6. Major Meggs; 7. Unknown; 8. Billy Winne, the penny postman; 9-10. Unknown; 11. Thurlow Weed, politician and journalist; 12. Unknown; 13. Ex-Governor Joseph C. Yates; 14-15. Unknown.

William Henry Brown (1808-1882), born in South Carolina, began to cut profiles early in his life and in 1824, at sixteen years of age, he made a profile of General Lafayette while that notable was visiting in Philadelphia. Brown was a scissor silhouettist who specialized in cutting rather complicated pieces such as funeral processions and fire brigades, one of which was 25 feet long. He used touches of gilding and color sparingly, and his portraits of men were unsurpassed for vividness and accuracy.

Silhouette of DeWitt Clinton and coaches (1831), 81" x 19", paper pasted on cotton, William H. Brown. Courtesy, Connecticut Historical Society, Hartford.

This stone building at Alcove, built in the early 1800's in the Federal style, is a part of the original grist mill complex that spanned the elbow of the Hannacroix Creek.

Stone mill building (ca. 1800), Alcove.

There is an interesting map which survives that depicts the settlement at Alcove, begun in 1790 when Casparus Ackerman erected a grist mill beside the Hannacroix Creek. This mill was later owned by Archibald Stephens and then in 1885 by W. S. Briggs. Originally, the settlement was named Stephensville, in honor of the mill owner, but the name of Alcove was given to the hamlet when the post office was established in 1881.

The mansion house shown on the map, along with its many outbuildings, built ca.1820, was the property of the prosperous mill owner Archibald Stephens. Stephens was the Supervisor of the Town of Coeymans in 1818. His farmhouse and many others, along with the entire village of Indian Fields, was demolished and the land flooded for the Alcove Reservoir, constructed in 1928 to supply water for the city of Albany.

John Preston, the surveyor and draftsman of this map, was undoubtedly the school teacher from Van Leuven's Corners, located in the northwest section of the Town of Westerlo, along the Delaware Turnpike (Route 85). He was a man of many talents, keeping a tavern, operating a tannery and curry shop and serving as a school teacher. He was also the author of a mathematics textbook printed in Albany in 1834, by G. J. Lomis of 9 Washington Street.

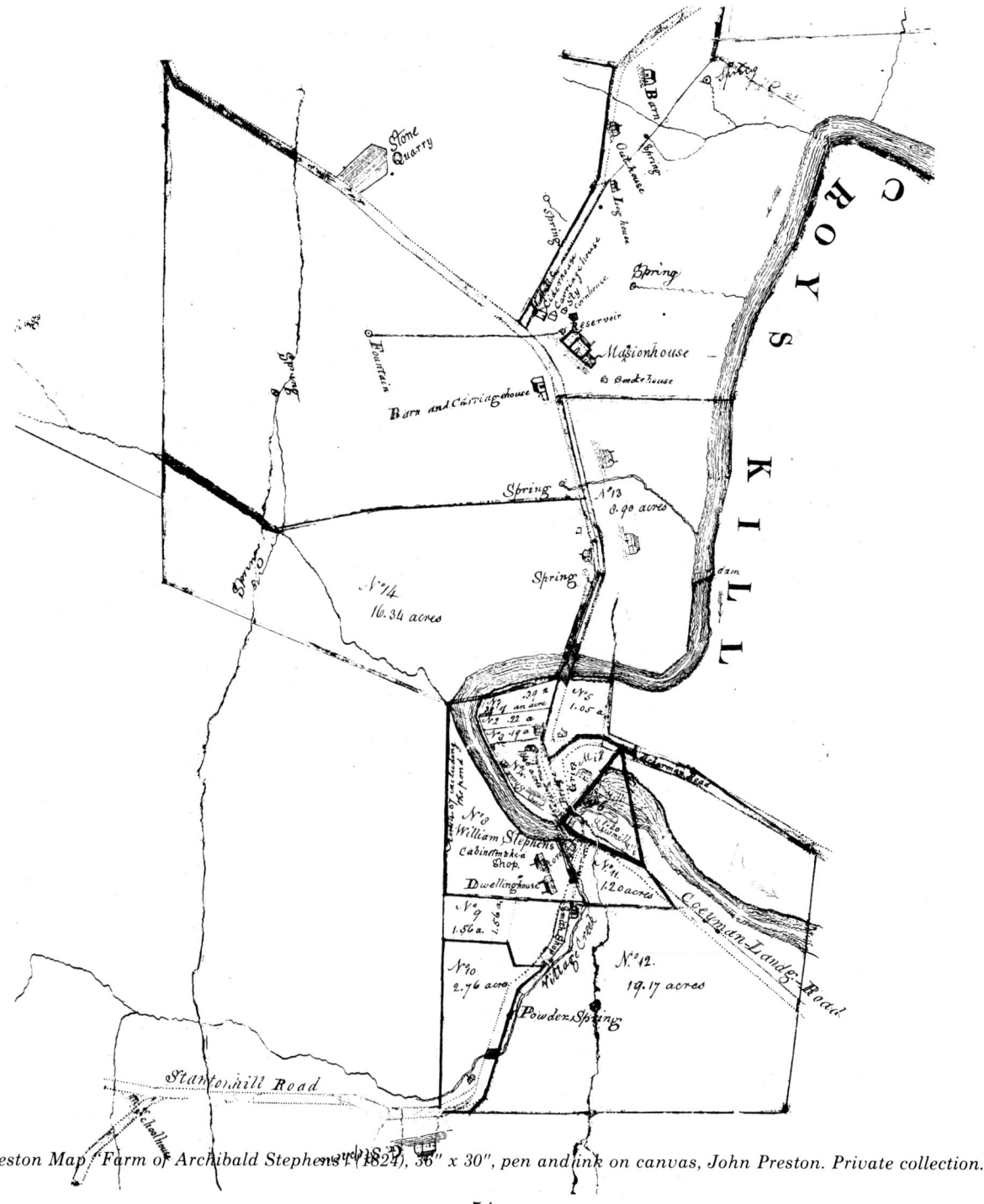

Preston Map, "Farm of Archibald Stephens" (1824), 36" x 30", pen and ink on canvas, John Preston. Private collection.

Weapons of War from Watervliet

With the purchase of 12 acres of land in 1813 in Gibbonsville (Watervliet), the Federal government created the Watervliet Arsenal to supply ammunition, harnesses and gun carriages to troops fighting the British on the western and northern frontiers of New York State. It is the nation's oldest arsenal. The Erie Canal, finished in 1825, ran through the Arsenal enclosure and provided water power for the gun shops and also convenient transportation, making the property valuable to the War Department.

Over the years, more land was acquired and new buildings constructed, including the East Powder Magazine, built in 1828, with walls of stone four feet thick. This is the oldest building in the Arsenal compound.

The Commander's residence known as *Quarters One* was built in 1842 and has been continuously occupied by the Commanders of the Arsenal. Stephen Vincent Benét (1898-1943), distinguished American poet and author, wrote the greater part of his first published novel "The Beginnings of Wisdom", while residing here when his father, Colonel J. Walker Benét, was Arsenal Commander from 1919-1921. The house is a modified Greek Revival style with walls of gray trimmed Canajoharie limestone of two foot thickness. The front entrance portico is flanked by Doric columns and an entablature above, with flat columns on each corner of the house. The porches were a later addition.

Until the 19th century, building materials had always been worked by hand. The potential of using iron in architectural structures began to be realized by the 1850's, and the fabrication of building components in cast iron was a revolution in construction techniques. The speed of construction and its lower cost compared to stone contributed to its adoption. The Iron Building was erected in 1859 to meet the need for a fireproof storage area at the Arsenal. The building was cast in sections by the Badger Architectural Iron Works, New York City, and was shipped by barge up the Hudson and assembled on its present site. It is an early example of prefabricated construction that is still used in part in its original capacity as a storehouse. All the principal structural elements, bearing walls, columns and beams, and all exterior surfaces except the roof are of cast iron. The roof trusses are wrought iron, as are the interior stairways. This sturdy building has classical architectural details, transferred from stone to cast iron.

Powder Magazine, Watervliet Arsenal (1828). Courtesy, Department of the Army.

Quarters #1, Watervliet Arsenal (1842), Courtesy, Department of the Army.

Cast-iron building, Watervliet Arsenal (1859). Courtesy, Department of the Army.

During the Civil War, the Watervliet Arsenal was kept in round-the-clock production to meet the demands for ordnance supplies, including gun carriages, cartridge boxes and accoutrements for cavalry horses. After the War, the Arsenal became a storage depot, until it was selected by the Army in 1887 for conversion to cannon production. With the advent of the Spanish-American War in 1898, the Watervliet Arsenal was able to produce the nation's first 16-inch gun.

Time and again the Arsenal has faced lean years of inactivity and rumors of closing. There seems to be little likelihood of this at present, as it plays a major role in research and development of cannon, mortars and recoilless rifles, to complement its manufacturing mission. It has been, since its inception, important to the economic activity of Albany County.

Communal Living - The Watervliet Shakers

In the quest for perfection in this life and a place where they could practice their own form of Godly worship, Mother Ann Lee (1736-1784) in 1776, led her handful of followers to settlement on a boggy farm of 200 acres in the countryside of Albany County, about six miles north of the city. This spot marked the beginnings of the Shaker movement in America, known as The United Society of Believers in Christ's Second Appearing. Mother Ann Lee was the spiritual leader, considered the female counterpart of Jesus, in this Protestant religious communal society, which among other things practiced celibacy, and consecration of their time and talent to the glory of God. By the most diligent labor, they converted the soggy farmland into abundantly productive acreage. By prophecy and proselytizing, they converted many adults and adopted children, generally orphans, to be followers of their faith. They founded not only the colony at Watervliet, but several others in various sections of the country. At their height, about 1850, the Shakers numbered approximately 6000 members, mainly in the Northeast. After the Civil War, all Shaker communities went into a gradual decline. The last Shaker left Watervliet for the settlement at New Lebanon, N.Y., in July 1938.

At the high point of their prosperity at Watervliet, circa 1840, there were four "families", in total about 350 people, living on over 3000 acres.

Each family managed its own affairs and had its own spiritual and governmental leaders, composed of both men and women of the order. The Watervliet Shakers lived in groups of buildings composed of *North, South, West* and *Church* families. The Church Family section is now occupied by the Albany County Ann Lee Home complex; the North Family buildings were burned by fire in 1927 and again in 1932. Their land is now occupied by the Shaker Ridge Country Club. The West and South Family buildings are privately owned and occupied. The buildings and most of the 770 acres of land that still remain, as well as the Shaker cemetery, have been placed on the National Register. The burying ground contains neat rows of simple white headstones, all identical, except one that is a bit larger - this stone commemorates the resting place of Mother Ann.

We admire the Shakers for their devotion to God and their tenacity to their religious beliefs, their neatness and devotion to industry; for their handicrafts, which exhibit a serene, simple beauty; for their inventions which were years ahead of their time, and for their skill in many forms of agriculture. Their dwellings and outbuildings were simple, clean-lined and sturdy. Their excellent farm produce found a ready market in Albany and their garden seeds, patent medicines, canned fruits and vegetables were shipped around the world.

A photographic view of the Church family community, taken in 1927, shows the main dwelling house of wood, with its bell tower, built in 1818. The 19th century stone building to the left was the sisters' workshop and beside it was a wooden dwelling house of 1790. On the right of the picture in the foreground is the new meeting house, built in 1846, the first meeting house of 1791 and the brick ministry house built in 1825. The meeting house of 1846 has been faced with brick and now serves as a Catholic chapel for the Ann Lee Home facility.

Panorama of Watervliet Church Family community. Courtesy, Shaker Museum, Old Chatham.

The West Family granary is one of the few Shaker outbuildings still in existence on the Watervliet properties. It has been converted into a residence.

West Family Granary, Watervliet (19th century). Courtesy, Shaker Museum, Old Chatham.

"The Plan of Watervliet, N.Y." is a large map that may have been drawn in 1839 by David Austin Buckingham, a member of the Watervliet Shaker community at that time.

A portion of the map shows the buildings and grounds of the *1st Order* which was known also as *The Church Family*. The diagram illustrates the first meetinghouse as a gambrel-roofed structure, drawn at right and below the dwelling house. This meeting house was built in 1791 for the Watervliet Church Family by Brother Moses Johnson of Enfield, New Hampshire. The ministry house, built in 1825, is to the right of the dwelling house, above the meeting house. It is still standing, as is the brick trustee's office at the lower right (1830) and the center building on the left, the brick shop, built in 1822. These buildings are now a part of the facilities of the Albany County Ann Lee Home.

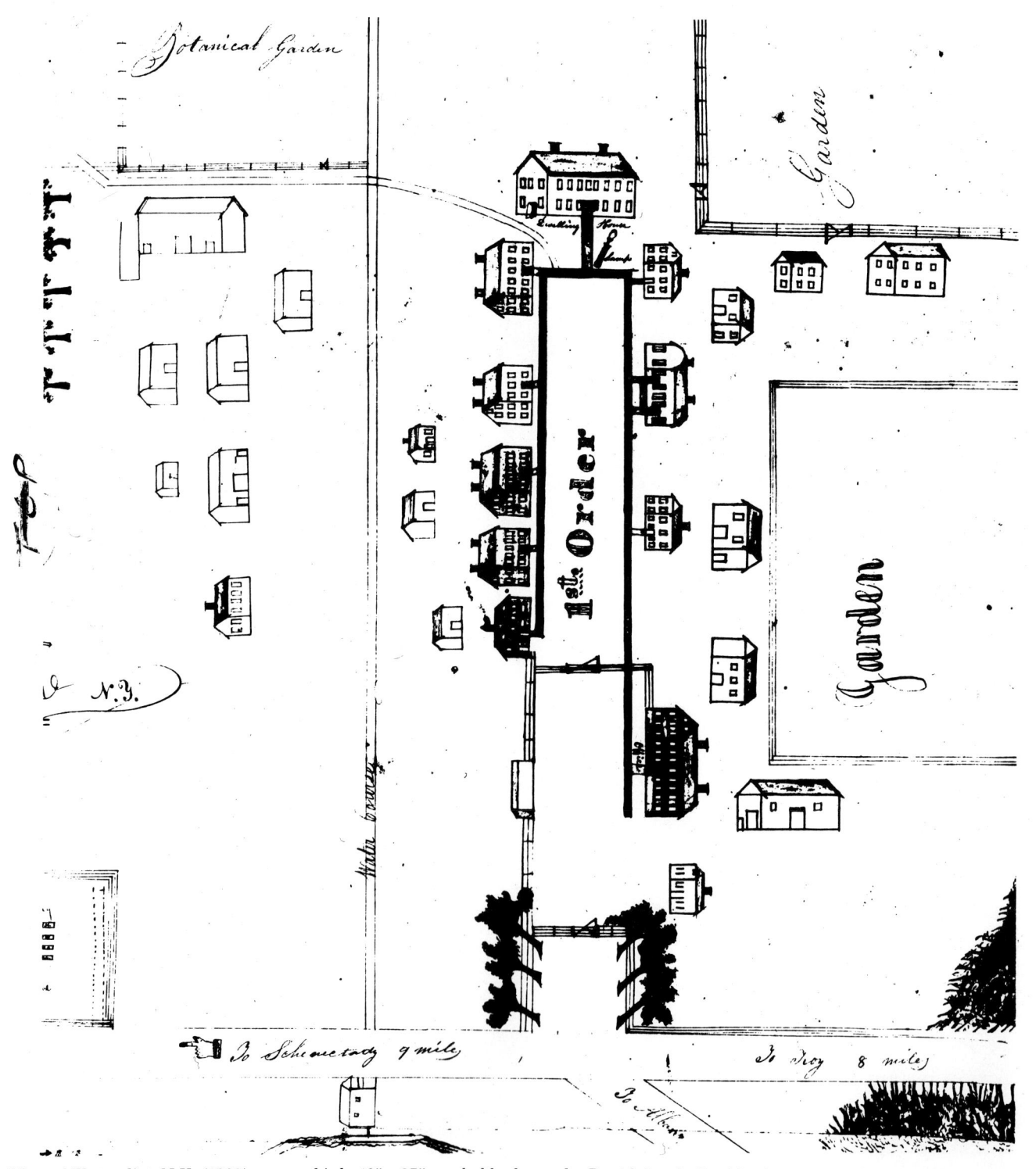

Plan of Watervliet, N.Y. *(1839), pen and ink, 48" x 27", probably drawn by David Austin Buckingham, a member of the Watervliet Shaker community. From collection of Albany Institute of History and Art. Photo courtesy, Town of Colonie.*

A Crossroad of Commerce - Banks and Bankers

The first serious discussions about founding a bank in Albany County were held in 1792. A group of gentlemen who represented the expanding business interests in the area promoted the need for a bank in the northern section of the State and proposed the issue of stock in the "Albany Bank". When the books were opened for subscriptions a week later, the stock was taken up in less than three hours. The Legislature gave the Albany Bank its charter, after considerable opposition from the New York City faction, and Abraham Ten Broeck was the first president. This bank existed for 70 years, but poor business conditions and financial panics at the time of the Civil War forced the bank to close its doors in 1861, along with four other Albany banks.

From its inception, some of the city merchants had felt that the Albany Bank was not cognizant of their interests, and so in 1803, they organized the New York State Bank, again after much opposition in the Legislature. Bank charters in this period were often a source of controversy and usually closely associated with political factions. Elkanah Watson, a New Englander who was convinced that New York State and Albany in particular presented the greatest opportunities for growth, especially in land speculation, had settled in the city in 1789. He was a promotor with vision and he quickly became a leading citizen. Elected to the first board of directors of the Albany Bank, within a year he was out, probably because of differences of opinion with the Dutch directors and stockholders. He left Albany for a time but in 1803 was back, championing the cause of the merchants. He became the principal promotor of the second bank, and largely through his efforts the New York State Bank came into being.

The New York State Bank made its first loan to help finance the Great Western Turnpike Company, and in 1822 helped insure the success of the Erie Canal project when it gave large loans to the Canal Fund. It gave support to the first passenger railroad between Albany and Schenectady, helped new settlers with financing their farms and assisted merchants with the establishment of new businesses. It is still in existence today under the name of The State Bank of Albany, 69 State Street.

John Taylor (ca. 1804), oil on canvas, 29¾" x 23¾", Ezra Ames. Courtesy, Albany Institute of History and Art.

The portrait of John Taylor (1742-1829) first president of the New York State Bank, was painted by Ezra Ames in 1804. It is a realistic, carefully drawn portrait of the bank president, surrounded by books and a stack of carefully tied notes, which indicate his pursuits. Taylor had a varied career as an Indian translator, delegate to the Provincial Congress, Assemblyman, Senator, Lieutenant Governor, Chancellor of the Board of Regents and Bank President.

State Bank of Albany and State Street (north side) as it appeared in 1804, watercolor on paper, 1850, James Eights. Courtesy, State Bank of Albany.

The lot where the bank building stands was purchased in 1804 from Isaiah Townsend. The leading architect of Albany, Philip Hooker, was commissioned to design a bank building, the front of which has since been incorporated into the larger 16-story building erected in 1927-28. The details of the original two-story building included, on the ground floor, two arched entranceways flanking a central window that repeated the Palladian motif of the window above. A triangular pediment enriched with a swagged garland, surmounted by carved urns above the second story, completed the elevation. In the James Eights watercolor of the State Bank and that portion of State Street that adjoins it, we find the artist portraying a vivid picture of buildings and people in the city of Albany in the early part of the 19th century. James Eights (1791-1882) was born in Albany. He is best known for his series of views of Albany, but he was also a naturalist, physician and explorer. He was a scientific artist for the Erie Canal geological survey and for the geological report on New York State made by Ebenezer Emmons, an associate of Eights.

Other banks were established rapidly over the years as the need for them increased with the rising prosperity of the city and county. Albany's banks became the depository for funds from the municipality, the State and Federal governments. At the present time, Albany is the leading financial center of upstate New York and, in the development of commerce and industry within the county, banks and bankers have played a key role.

Portrait Painter of Albany

The Revolution had put an end forever to the aristocratic ideal that rank and birth were the only attributes necessary for advancement in society. A new spirit of republican liberalism gave emphasis to a feeling of respect for the common man. American art work at this time began to assume a national style that expressed this search for new ideals, with the desire to emulate the integrity and nobility of the heroes of the Greek and Roman republics. Even though the painters wanted to develop a completely new style of painting, the paradox was that these painters of the early Republic, such as Trumbell, Peale and Stuart, had to lean on roots of classical inspiration because they had not had a chance to broaden their own horizons. While they did not hark back to the strict theme of a style based upon antique sculpture and classical art objects for use in their paintings, as did the painters in Europe, they applied the ideals of ancient virtues to their own form of neo-classical painting. They saw a world of noble actions and devotion to duty that could be transferred to historical canvasses of events that had formed the new nation, and that were exemplified in portraits of America's national heroes. In Albany, Ezra Ames became renowned as a portrait painter who made excellent likenesses of local people of importance.

Ezra Ames (1769-1836) was born in Massachusetts, but by the age of 25 had decided to move to New York State. In 1793, he inserted an advertisement in an Albany newspaper, announcing that he was ready to begin business as an artist. Although at first he did not receive any portrait commissions, he does list receipts for the painting of signs, sleighs, buckets, a table and two chests and a Masonic apron. It was not long before his artistic skill brought him patrons for portraits and miniatures. In 1794, he married Zipporah Wood of Massachusetts and in that same year he joined the Masonic Order in Albany. This was the beginning of a long time interest and many advancements in the field of Freemasonry, which eventually led to national recognition, as he served as Master of the Grand Lodge of the State for 24 years. This connection also gave him extensive employment as a painter of Masonic regalia and engraver of their medals and certificates.

Ezra Ames - Self Portrait (ca. 1800), oil on canvas, 30½" x 24½". Courtesy, Albany Institute of History and Art.

Ames' daughter, Maria Lucretia, married the Reverend William James (1797-1868), a Presbyterian minister and son of William James Sr., in 1824. William James the elder (1771-1832) was an Irishman who arrived in Albany in 1793, the same year as Ezra Ames. He established himself as a commission merchant, and he also made a fortune in landholding and real estate. In time, he became the second wealthiest man in the State. He was the grandfather of William James (1842-1910), the philosopher, and Henry James (1843-1916), the novelist.

William James, Sr. *(ca. 1827), oil on wood panel, 29½" x 23½", Ezra Ames. Union College Collection.*

Mrs. William James *(ca. 1827), oil on wood panel, 29½" x 23½", Ezra Ames. Courtesy, Albany Institute of History and Art.*

The earliest painting efforts of Ames were compositions that had a primitive quality. His technique improved over the years as he trained himself by making copies after portraits by Copley and Stuart. The influence of Stuart in particular is apparent in many of his portraits, especially in his use of classical architecture for background, coupled with the use of books and documents.

The portrait of William James of Albany, holding a letter in his hand dated 1822 and sitting before a background of classical column and drapery is illustrative of Ames' use of these features, and the pose as well is copied from some of Stuart's portraits. It is a forthright portrait of the wealthy commission merchant of Albany.

Very often in his portraits of women, a shawl with a flowered band would be draped about their shoulders. In his portrait of Mrs. William James, a thin, filmy white shawl is draped about her shoulders and the lace collar and wisps of hair are carefully delineated. Ames' later paintings became accomplished works of art, with advances in technique and characterization clearly expressed by these two portraits.

While painters of Ames' generation were working mainly in portraits, the *Romantic Landscape* is one of a very few landscapes that he painted. Its vaporous quality anticipated the later romantic Hudson River School of painting, with its allegorical landscape of romantic castles and emphasis on wildlife and foliage.

Ezra Ames' home and shop were located for many years at 41 South Pearl Street. He was active in the Albany Mechanics Society, as was Benjamin Knower, the banker, Philip Hooker, the architect, and Isaac Hutton, a silversmith. In 1814 Ames entered the banking business when elected a Director of the Mechanics and Farmers Bank. Twenty years later he was president of that institution. Of his three avocations - painting, Freemasonry and banking, he reached the pinnacle in each.

Lady of the Lake, *allegorical landscape, oil on canvas, 45½" x 34½", Ezra Ames. Courtesy, Albany Institute of History and Art.*

Nathaniel Adams *(first quarter of 19th century), unknown artist. Private collection.*

Mrs. Nathaniel Adams *(first quarter of 19th century), unknown artist. Private collection.*

Everyone in town and country could not afford to have his portrait painted by Ezra Ames, who charged $25 for a bust portrait. Even that well-known artist had competition in a city the size of Albany and also from itinerant painters who stopped for short intervals in the larger villages. It is not known who painted the portraits of Nathanial Adams (1802-1892) and his wife, Rhogenia Baumes Adams (1806-1861), but he certainly was a talented painter who gave good delineation to the faces of his subjects as well as to their costumes.

We first find mention of Nathaniel Adams in the 1825 City Directory of Albany, where he is listed as having a porter, oyster and victualling cellar at State and Market Streets and a house at 138 State Street. It is probable that he was one of the many New Englanders who made their way to Albany County in the late 18th and early 19th centuries. By 1833, the building in which he conducted his business was known as the *Museum Building* because Henry Trowbridge conducted a museum of natural curiosities therein. The building was owned by Thorpe and Sprague and was the starting place for their stage coaches. In 1835, the Directory lists Adams as running the Marble Pillar Refectory in the basement story of the Museum, with his house at 42 South Pearl Street. In 1839 he still was listed at Marble Pillars but had a house in Bethlehem and by 1841 he was just listed as residing at Bethlehem. Of course, by this time he had built the inn on the Delaware Turnpike in Bethlehem, which until recently served as the Bethlehem Town Hall in the village of Delmar.

Miniatures are nothing more than small portraits, painted with exactness and refinement, in transparent watercolor, usually on a small, thin piece of ivory. The laying on of color by the technique of stippling and hatching in minute and dextrous manner is the trademark of the miniaturist. Miniatures were intimate personal tokens of affection, which would aid the recipient in visualizing the subject, and were meant to be worn on the person, set into a small snuff or jewel box or kept in some small place such as a desk drawer.

Anson Dickinson, who started work as a silversmith and later studied drawing, was known to be painting miniatures in Albany from 1805-1810. He was highly talented and worked in almost monochromatic color, giving sensitivity to his subjects. The miniatures of Mr. and Mrs. Leonard Gansevoort are by Dickinson. William Dunlap was also a miniaturist working in Albany in the early years of the nineteenth century.

By 1850 the artist who painted in miniature no longer could compete with the accuracy and cheapness of the daguerreotype.

Miniatures of Mr. and Mrs. Leonard Gansevoort, 2¾" x 2⅛", ivory, Anson Dickinson. Courtesy, Albany Institute of History and Art.

The Albany painter Ezra Ames also painted in miniature. His daughter, Marcia Ames, was portrayed by him in 1820, holding a book and with a ruffled collar and sleeve emphasizing a flesh-toned dress.

Miniature of Marcia Ames (1820), 3¼" x 2¾", watercolor on paper, Ezra Ames. Courtesy, Albany Institute of History and Art.

Folk Perspectives in Art

Much of the population enjoyed what the folk artists of their time could produce - it was the art of the common people. Folk painting was a simple, unsophisticated approach to artistic expression, more typical in rural than urban areas. Folk painters responded to the sense of individualism, the cultural attitudes and values held by rural America. The folk artist painted portraits, landscapes and genre scenes that were a record of their times. They also decorated utilitarian objects such as coaches, signs, household furniture and utensils and walls and floors. Needlework and some sculpture also are forms of folk art.

Folk painters were not academic artists, but many probably had some painterly training from an art instructor. They also were influenced by imported prints and drawings and by painting and drawing manuals. In the later 19th century, many art instruction books were published for use in home and school.

The folk artist tried to approximate the visible appearance of things in a direct and colorful manner, often incorporating strong design and interesting details, but the artist often had limited technical abilities, as seen in the *Nathan Hawley and Family* portrait, painted by William Wilkie. This watercolor is one of the most important pieces of American folk art because of its depiction of the interior of a home of the period. It is characteristic of folk art because of the manner in which the family members were presented. The artist was not capable of drawing children and so the children in the painting look like miniature adults. According to family tradition, Nathan Hawley was the keeper of the city jail at Albany and William Wilkie was a prisoner in that jail.

Nathan Hawley and Family *(1801), watercolor on paper, 20" x 15¾", William Wilkie. Courtesy, Albany Institute of History and Art.*

In the drawing of Miss Elizabeth A. Vanderzee of New Baltimore, the artist used repetitive motifs to create decorative patterns and painted with clear outlines and bright colors. However, the forms are flat, without shadows, and the pose static. Elizabeth Vanderzee was the child of Albert Vanderzee (d. 1822) and his wife Catherine Van Slyke (d. 1832). Elizabeth married Thomas Houghtaling (1791-1869). The village of New Baltimore was settled by members of the Vanderzee family and is presently in Greene County. However, at the time the portrait of Elizabeth was made it was a part of Albany County, being set off from Albany in 1811.

Elizabeth A. Vanderzee *(1794), watercolor on paper, 13½" x 9½", unknown artist. Private collection.*

Mourning Picture *(19th century), silk thread on silk material, watercolor, 23" x 17", attributed to Garritje Van Wie. Courtesy, Albany County Historical Association.*

Mourning art was done in America before 1800, but it did not become popular until after Washington's death in 1799. The desire to memorialize the national hero helped create the fashion for the mourning picture that was soon being made to memorialize friends and loved ones. The mourning tribute not only expressed sentiment and respect for departed family members - it also reflected a personal closeness to religious thought and a reality of the nearness and often the suddenness, of death.

Most mourning pictures contain traditional Christian symbols of mourning such as the classical sarcophagus; the funerary urn — suggestive of containing the departed spirit; the willow tree, which symbolized the power of regrowth after being cut down and the flowing stream, which suggested cleansing waters. All of these were incorporated in an imaginary landscape of a garden-like setting, reflecting the neo-classic romantic interest in nature and also the Christian vision of Resurrection. The mourning figure(s) was an important element of the composition and was most often a lady, with head meekly bowed in grief, often leaning against the tomb and dressed in a Grecian style gown, indicative of the new classical fashion. The importance of the church in the lives of the mourner and the departed was expressed in the frequent representation and also the size in which the church structures were depicted. Sometimes dwelling houses or other architectural structures would be included.

These mourning pictures most often were worked in embroidery and paint on silk material and were meant to be hung in the Federal parlor. They usually were executed by young ladies of the middle class who had been taught the arts of painting and embroidery in private seminaries and finishing schools. By 1840, the art was degenerating into a morbid sentimentality and by mid-century it had all but disappeared. This was coincidental with the local church burying ground being replaced gradually by the public cemetery.

Very little is known about the origin of the mourning picture that is hanging in a bedroom of the Ten Broeck Mansion, but it probably has an Albany County origin. Records indicate that Garritje Van Wie did the needlework, which is silk thread on silk. She probably also painted in the face, arms and the sky background of the picture. The initials on the plinth are in script.

The art of silhouette cutting came to America from France; Augustin Edouart (1788-1861) was one of the most active cutters to come to America. Albany had several silhouette cutters practising their trade here in the early years of the 19th century, among them William Henry Brown, Thomas P. Jones, Louis Lemet, A. Janes, Timothy Gladding, Masters Hubard and Hankes and Master K. T. Nellis. R. Letton, proprietor of the Albany Museum, also did silhouette cutting.

Most silhouettes are simple, shadow profile portraits, in earlier times called "shades". They were cut either by hand or machine or painted in India ink and then pasted to a plain or painted background. In general, the hair and costume details were added with pencil or ink. One way of cutting silhouettes was for the artist to use a *Physiognotrace*, or profile machine. In this process, the person having his likeness done would sit behind a light, which reflected the image onto a sheet of thin paper, held in the shadow-box machine. The artist would pencil in the outline, and a pantograph instrument reduced the larger head to 2 or 3 inches in size. These profiles were then cut with sharp scissors or a penknife. The profile machine also would be used to trace the profile on white paper, after which the artists would cut the hollow out and mount it on dark paper to get what was known as a "hollow-cut" silhouette.

Silhouettes also were cut directly by hand. This was accomplished with great rapidity and precision by the artists. Sometimes silhouettes were painted on glass. Family groups were a popular subject for silhouette cutting, but these are more rare than the single portrait.

Maria Houghtaling silhouette (19th century), cut paper and ink, 5" x 4", unknown artist. Private collection.

Anthony Houghtaling silhouette (19th century), cut paper and ink, 5" x 4", unknown artist. Private collection.

In the silhouettes of Anthony and Maria Van Bergen Houghtaling, the hair and costume have been drawn in with ink. Anthony Houghtaling (b. 1793) was the grandson of Thomas Houghtaling (1731-1824), who purchased a large tract of land known as the Houghtaling Patent in the Coxsackie-New Baltimore area and married Elizabeth Witbeck (1739-1820), daughter of Andries Witbeck of Aquetuck. Anthony's wife, Maria Van Bergen (1795-1823), was from the family of that name in the Coxsackie area. Their daughter, Sarah Ann Houghtaling (1821-1874), married Fletcher Blaisdell of Coeymans in 1838. It was in that year that Fletcher built the Blaisdell family home on Westerlo Street in the village of Coeymans.

Educational Endeavors

The need for educating the majority of the people of New Netherland never had been felt to any great extent during the colonial period. The Patroon's Charter had stipulated that a minister and a schoolmaster be provided for the settlers, but though there is mention of a schoolmaster at Fort Orange in 1639, there is little mention of schools or teachers in the early records. Books were brought over from Europe and the Dutch produced very little writing among themselves - they seemed more interested in trade and commerce than in books. The average Dutch farmer in New Netherland could neither read nor write, and those in authority were quite indifferent to the matter. The ministers received their education in Holland and sometimes they also served as schoolmaster. In their teaching, the Reformed Church Cathechism was the first course of instruction, with reading and writing secondary. Of course, the wealthy employed private tutors for their children, but there was little interest in the cause of public education and very little money expended upon it.

Joseph Henry statue (1928), John Flanigan. Academy Park, Albany.

When the English took over the province, they recognized the need for teaching English to certain of the inhabitants. Some efforts were made to establish schools, but little legislation was passed for this purpose. By the time of the Revolution, the schools that existed were few in number, the teachers not well equipped, the buildings of a makeshift character and the equipment meager. There were some private schools taught by individuals or church societies. Only with the advent of New Englanders coming into the area, did people begin to insist that part of their tax money go for the cause of public elementary education. The common school system grew out of legislation of 1789 in which two lots in each township were set aside from the public lands for gospel and school purposes. In 1795, the Legislature appropriated monies for the general support of common schools, with money being divided among the counties based on their legislative representation.

Attempts had been made in Albany from as early as 1785 to establish an academy, but no definite results were forthcoming until 1813 when a Board of Trustees was appointed to apply for a charter to the Regents. The charter was granted and in that same year, the Albany Academy came into being. The cornerstone of its building, designed by Philip Hooker, was laid in 1815, and it is one of only three buildings by Hooker still remaining in the city. In the Academy's arched windows and pilastered, paneled walls there is a similarity in style to the City Hall in New York. A Frenchman, Joseph Mangin, is credited with the design of that work, along with John Macomb, and Philip Hooker may have been inspired by their design. The bold carving of the interior woodwork is characteristic of the craftsmen that Hooker favored, and combines refinement with bold decorative scale. The former chapel on the second floor, with its cove ceiling and Corinthian cornice and pilasters, is one of the great public rooms of its period.

Albany Academy (1815), Philip Hooker. Academy Park, Albany. Courtesy, New York State Department of Commerce.

In the Albany Academy building, Joseph Henry (1799-1878), in 1830, invented an electro-magnet telegraph instrument that transmitted an audible sound, thus making his name forever famous in the scientific world.

He was born in Albany, the son of William Henry, a Scottish laborer. His father died when he was nine and his maternal grandmother made a home for him in Galway for a time, but as a young man he came back to Albany. His aunt, Elizabeth Henry, had married James Selkirk, a Revolutionary War veteran, in the First Presbyterian Church of Albany in 1787. The Selkirks and Henrys had come from Scotland on the same ship. Young Joseph Henry taught for two years in the one room school at Selkirk to earn money for furthering his education. It is probable that he lived with his aunt Elizabeth in her brick cottage, which is still standing in the village of Selkirk.

By hard work, Joseph Henry built a fund for his education and attended the Albany Academy. He also raised the needed tuition for night school by tutoring in the family of Stephen Van Rensselaer and assisting Dr. T. Romeyn Beck, principal of the Albany Academy. Beck recognized Henry's abilities and offered him encouragement and support. In 1826, Joseph Henry was named to the chair of mathematics at the Academy. His teaching schedule was supplemented by scientific experiments after hours. In his crude laboratory at the Academy building, he pursued the study of electricity and discovered the principles of electromagnetic self-induction, from which came the dynamo and the electric motor. While at the Academy, he also served as private tutor to Henry James, son of William James. Henry James later became the father of the philosopher, William James and the novelist, Henry James. Joseph Henry was also the Librarian of the Albany Institute and often presented papers to the society on his scientific experiments.

In 1832, Henry was elected to the chair of natural philosophy at Princeton University and in 1846, he became the first secretary and director of the Smithsonian Institution in Washington. He carried out research that resulted in the formation of the United States Weather Bureau. Joseph Henry died in Washington, D.C. in 1878, but his statue in Academy Park in Albany perpetuates the memory of his achievements in Albany County.

The Political Perspective

The 4th Provincial Congress (N.Y.) was elected immediately after the Declaration of Independence and declared the state independent on July 9, 1776. Despite the tempestuous times of battle in New York in 1776-77, by April of 1777, a constitution was adopted for the state on the authority of the State Convention. The colonial Assembly had given the colonists familiarity with governmental procedures, as had the provincial congresses and committees preceding the Revolutionary War. In the new constitution, there was judicial provision and the Senate and Assembly were composed in much the same way as they are today, with senatorial districts and an allocated quota of assemblymen. Since there was a distrust of executive authority as it had been represented in the colonial governors, there were some restrictions placed on the governor's power. In order to vote for governor and senators, a person had to be a white male and own property valued at 100 pounds or more. Certain merchants and artisans, who paid for the right to do business in the cities, and a percentage of smaller property owners, could vote for assemblymen. Thus the new constitution was restrictive with regard to those who could cast a vote, but it did contain democratic principles, such as freedom of religion and trial by jury.

George Clinton was elected the first governor in 1777 and was re-elected to that post for 18 years. His election was one indication of the end of decision making in the Assembly by the old aristocratic land-holding families, who had previously held most of the 28 seats in the Provincial Assembly of the colony. Clinton was well-to-do and had important connections, but he was considered to be a man of the people and he held their confidence.

Party politics emerged early in New York State and party organization reached a high point here, influencing the rest of the nation for a long period of years. Even the wealthy landowners had such diversity of background that they did not all congregate in one party. Two political factions emerged in New York at the time of the proposed ratification of the national constitution in 1787. Hamilton, the Schuylers and Livingstons urged its adoption, believing in a strong national government and the necessity for solidifying it, largely for the protection of their property. This group became a part of the newly formed *Federalist* party. Yet, there were many people who believed their rights and privileges could best be preserved by a strong state government and these powerful *Anti-Federalists*, led by George Clinton, proposed a Bill of Rights to be included within the constitution, and what they advocated was eventually adopted.

In 1795, George Clinton declined to run again for office and John Jay, chief justice of the U.S. under President Washington and one who had been influential in shaping the state constitution in 1777, was elected to the governorship. After this defeat, the Anti-Federalists, now beginning to be called *Republicans*, and claiming to represent the common people, worked to strengthen the party under the leadership of DeWitt Clinton (George Clinton's nephew) and Aaron Burr. Jay was a capable governor, but a series of blunders by the Federalists in charge of the national government gave the Republicans a victory and put George Clinton back at the head of state government in 1801.

Child's sleigh decorated with picture of Martin Van Buren. Inscribed: "Painted by Donald Fisher. Presented to William Cornell. By his Friend J. Brooks, Jr., Albany, N.Y. 1841". 29" x 13½". Courtesy, Columbia County Historical Association.

In spite of the Republican victories, there was a period of confusion in New York politics. Political controversy and feuding were strong in Albany County between 1801 and 1825, mainly among the Republicans. A group of malcontents within that party were instrumental in forming a small group in New York City in 1806 that came to be known as Tammany Hall, and eventually exercised great control in the political sphere in Albany.

The Federalists, in the meantime, were declining by 1800 and had crumbled as an organization by 1820, with some members shifting their support to the Republicans. DeWitt Clinton, largely because of his advocacy of the Erie Canal, was elected governor in 1817. Among the Republicans an anti-Clintonian faction arose under the leadership of a political genius, Martin Van Buren, of Kinderhook. This group was known as the Bucktails, so named because they wore deer tails in their hats at political functions. Two of Van Buren's stalwart supporters were William L. Marcy and Marcy's father-in-law, Benjamin Knower, of Albany and Guilderland. Van Buren was able to undermine Clinton and put into the State Senate a strong Bucktail opposition. Among the people a surge of democratic feeling, particularly for suffrage extension, prompted a new constitutional convention in Albany in 1821. Many significant changes were made in the state constitution, and the suffrage issue was probably the most important because it banished nearly all property qualifications for white male voters, thus shifting the balance of power in the Legislature forever from an elite corps of landholders to the common man.

By 1821, Van Buren, now a U.S. Senator, had obtained enough support to build his own political machine. The group of talented men he gathered about him became known as the *Albany Regency*, a powerful political organization within the state. Van Buren became governor in 1828, but resigned the next year to become Secretary of State under President Andrew Jackson, whom he followed to the president's chair in 1837.

George Clinton, *oil on canvas, 52" x 40", Ezra Ames. Courtesy, Albany Institute of History and Art.*

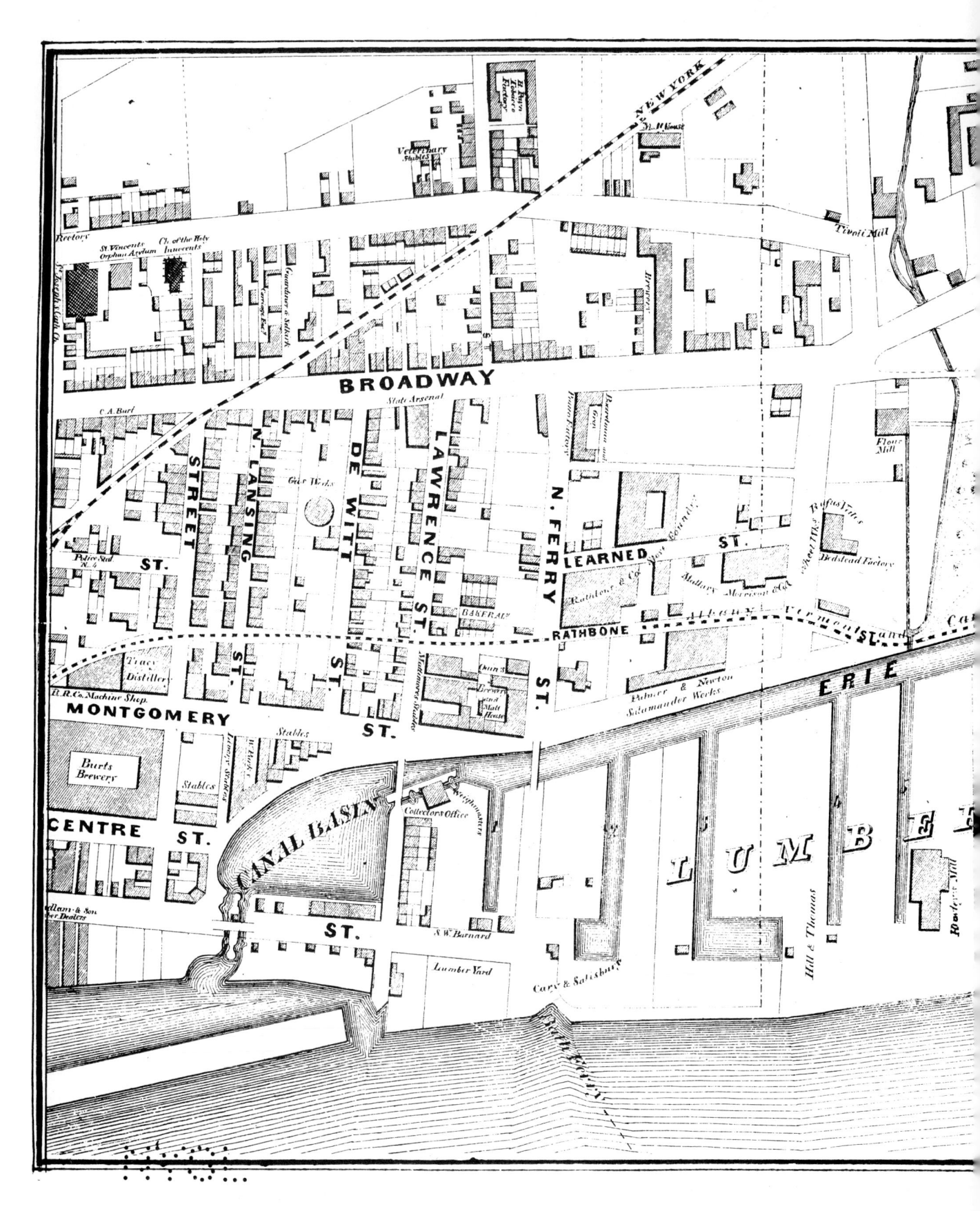

Albany Lumber District (1857), Hendrick Insurance Company. Courtesy, New York State Library.

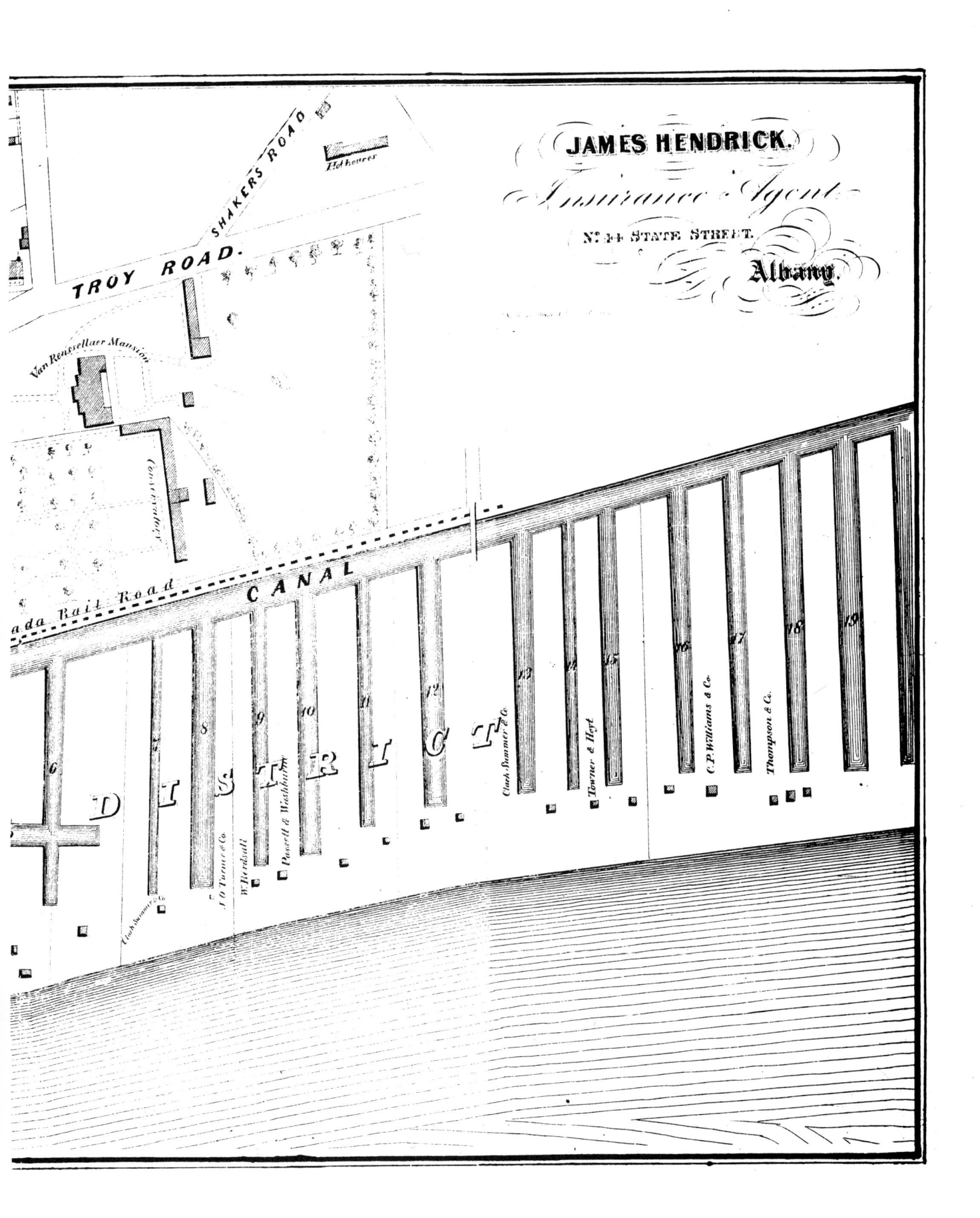

JAMES HENDRICK.
Insurance Agent
N.º 44 STATE STREET.
Albany.

TROY ROAD.
SHAKERS ROAD
Hot houses
Van Rensselaer Mansion
Conservatory
ada Rail Road
CANAL
DISTRICT
Clark Sammer & Co.
J.O. Turner & Co.
W. Birdsall
Pessett & Washburn
Clark Sammer & Co.
Towner & Hoyt
C.P. Williams & Co.
Thompson & Co.

ATTENTION!
ANTI-RENTERS!

AWAKE! AROUSE!

A Meeting of the friends of Equal Rights will be held on *Second Tuesday - February at Court House*

in the Town of *Bern —* at *1* O'clock.

Let the opponents of Patroonry rally in their strength. A great crisis is approaching. Now is the time to strike. The minions of Patroonry are at work. No time is to be lost. Awake! Arouse! and

> Strike 'till the last armed foe expires,
> Strike for your altars and your fires—
> Strike for the green graves of your sires,
> God and your happy homes!

☛ **The Meeting will be addressed by PETER FINKLE and other Speakers.**

Anti-Rent Poster (19th Century). Courtesy, New York State Library.

CHAPTER III

Coming of Age in Albany County ca. 1830-1900

Industrialization advanced steadily within the county during the 19th century, as technical knowledge and skill developed rapidly. The city of Albany had been, from 1686, a separate entity within the county. That did not mean, however, that its influence and prosperity had not spread throughout the county. Indeed, it had always provided a covenient and ready market for the farm produce of the county and many county residents had work in the city. Albany is important in this period of the 19th century for the number and importance of its manufacturing industries.

In the early 1800's, the iron industry had its beginnings in the county with the establishment of small foundaries and machine shops. Some of these developed into large businesses and a car wheel works was established by the Thatcher family in 1852 that for many years supplied wheels to the leading railroads of the country, including the New York Central. Albany was a leading center for the manufacture of iron stoves in the 19th century, production reaching a height of 220,000 stoves a year by 1888.

Lumber had been one of Albany County's earliest exports. This grew into a prominent factor in the commercial interests of the city and county with the opening of the Erie Canal. Lumber was brought here in such great quantities from the West and Canada that slips were cut from the canal on the northern edge of the city and lumber was stored along the banks of these slips. This area became known as the Lumber District and connected with this were numerous saw and planing mills. At this time, Albany was known as one of the largest lumber markets in the world. A period of depression in the later part of the century, as well as exhaustion of timber resources in the East and Great Lakes regions, led to the eventual decline of the lumber industry in Albany County.

A few years after settlement of the colony, breweries had been established and, with hops and barley growing areas nearby, the brewing industry in Albany County grew to immense proportions and contributed to the county's economy until recent years. In the 19th century, Albany was a principal center for meat processing, coffee and extract milling, machine shops, wire goods, furniture manufacture and law book publishing. The clay banks along the Hudson River provided an early start in the manufacture of bricks. This business grew rapidly and large brick works were established at Coeymans, North Coeymans and Cohoes. Another business that came to prominence and made fortunes for some residents of the county during the latter part of the century was "ice-harvesting" on the Hudson and on ponds made for that purpose. In the winter, the ice was cut into large blocks and stored in great wooden windowless ice houses that lined the banks of the river. In summer the ice was loaded onto barges and sent downstream to supply the homes, hotels and restaurants of New York City. Ice also was sent as far away as the West Indies, and to points along the East Coast. Before the days of the automobile, horses provided transportation within New York City. Great quantities of hay were needed to supply the livery stables there. The slopes of Albany County were ideal for the growing of hay and thousands of tons of hay were cut and shipped annually to New York, which contributed greatly to the county's economy.

All of the small manufacturing establishments along the creeks of the county that existed in the early part of the 19th century were to fall into disrepair and eventually fall away into ruin. These little mills were the victims of improvements in transportation and the consolidation of large factories in big cities. Farming was still pursued with vigor in the county, particularly dairy farming, the growing of fruits and vegetables and the breeding of livestock. The Civil War speeded up the economic growth of the northeast and hastened its change from an agrarian society into an urban, industrial society. Farming was arduous work and produce from the mid-west gave competition to local farmers. After the Civil War, many gave up their farms for easier and more profitable jobs in the manufacturing concerns in the city, and the county has seen a steady decline in farmland ever since. The year 1880 marked the peak of rural density of population, with growth thereafter shifting to urban areas.

Immigrants from Europe increased the population and fueled the industrial growth of Albany County greatly after 1820. Within a forty year span, five million newcomers had arrived at the Port of New York and many of them made their way to Albany County. The potato blight in Ireland caused many Irishmen to come to America and soon they were doing the hard work of digging the canals and building the railroads, while the women worked as household servants. The Dutch long before had given up contesting the New England emigrants and the transplanted New Englanders, in turn, became suspicious of the large numbers of Irish, who reached a high peak in the 1840's and 50's. By 1860, the Irish accounted for 40% of the population of the city of Albany. Germans fled political troubles at home to find opportunity in a new land. The movement of peoples from southern and eastern Europe, such as Italians, Greeks, Czechs and Poles, did not commence until the end of the 19th century. Many came to Albany County from Italy and found work as laborers on the burgeoning railroad facilities that were springing up in the county at that time.

In spite of the prosperity at mid-century, there were glaring disparities in the distribution of wealth and material benefits for many of the county's population. These immigrant people had to take the hardest jobs and live in the least desirable places. The local politicians helped them adjust to new ways, and in so doing secured their vote. The businessmen of the city saw them as potential customers. By the end of the 19th century, these "foreigners" had captured much political control and gained some economic power.

During this period, the county saw a revolution in economic activity that changed many of the old cultural and social values. Luxuries that had been reserved for the wealthy few of the county now became available to many more people. Good homes, a variety of occupations, education and art were available to those who had the desire and the enterprise to pursue them. The State government was just beginning to be a force that would help sustain the labor market from a broad area within the county in years to come. Eventually it would supplant the many manufacturing interests present in the city in the 19th century. The 20th century would be one of more transition, with new problems and new challenges for Albany County.

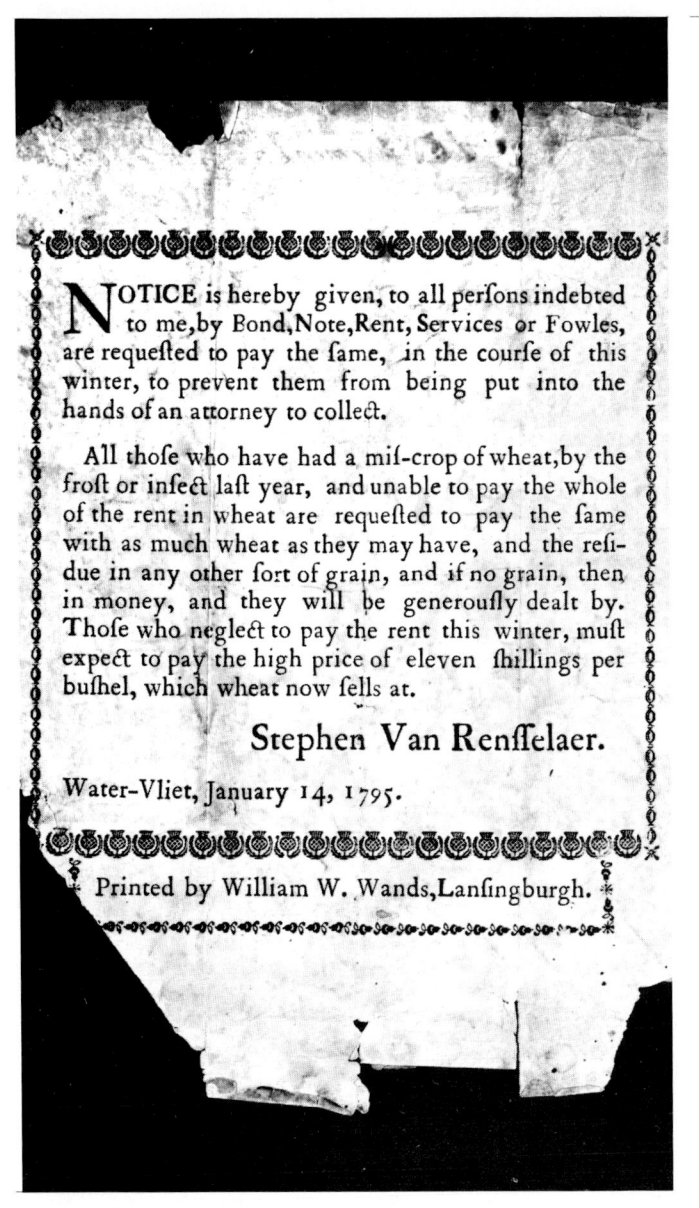

Rent Payment Notice (1795). Printed by William Wands for Stephen Van Rensselaer III. Courtesy, New York State Library.

Anti-Rentism — The Last Patroon

The phenomenon of anti-rentism especially raised its head in Albany County upon the death of the proprietor of the Manor of Rensselaerswyck, Stephen Van Rensselaer III, in 1839. Those who became settlers during his lifetime, like almost all previous settlers in Rensselaerswyck, held a rather vague title and possession of their farms on a *leasehold tenure*. This "lease" was quite different from the present usage of the word. The lease was a perpetual or "durable" lease, with the "Patroon" reserving to himself all mineral and water rights, and with the tenant paying certain feudal-type returns to the Patroon. Farmers on Van Rensselaer Manor often entered upon their farm without making any down payment and without paying rent for four to seven years. Thereafter, the farmer paid an annual rent in kind or money to the landlord. The tenant, if he wanted to dispose of the property, could not "sell" his farm but only the contract of incomplete sale, with its terms unaltered. This contract or lease also included the quarter-sale clause (the greatest cause of contention), whereby the Patroon reserved to himself one-quarter of the monies on every sale of a farm by a tenant.

By 1846, such leasehold farms in Albany County numbered 1,397 and yielded an annual rent of 23,390 bushels of wheat. Every New Year's Day, long lines of wagons came in from the country, loaded with wheat and chickens, to pay the rent, or with loads of wood, which generally were accepted in lieu of "one day's labor", also required by the leases. Stephen II had been known among the tenants as "The Good Patroon", for he had often been lax in collecting the rent, or letting rents run on indefinitely. There were arrears of about $400,000.00, many in the Helderberg section. Upon his death, his will directed that these rents be collected in order that his debts, amounting to about the same sum, might be paid and the estate be unencumbered.

When his heirs demanded these back rents and threatened eviction to those who did not pay, it aroused feelings of antagonism and led to open resistance by the tenants. Sheriffs came to the hill towns to serve writs of eviction against tenants in arrears. They were met by armed bands of tenants, masquerading as "Indians", with sheepskins pulled over their heads, wearing calico dresses and blowing tin horns in derision. After a few such confrontations, Governor Seward was forced to call out the Albany Militia. He requested the tenants not to resist the law, and being sympathetic to their cause, he pledged to go to the Legislature to effect a change. For the next few years, there were no encouraging results and scattered local resistance to the collection of rents went on. By 1844, the anti-rent movement had grown from a localized struggle and extended into several adjoining counties affected by the same system.

Anti-rent organizations were formed in all sections of the Manor by the tenants. Some of their leaders were men of intelligence and ability who organized conventions, published their own newspapers, and took the controversy to the political arena by electing their own spokesmen to the Legislature. Berne was for many years the capital of the Anti-Renters, for here and in neighboring areas lived the greatest number of people who were in resistance to the landlord. More leases were held in Berne than in any other township in Albany County. For these reasons, the Lutheran Church in Berne was chosen as the scene for a state anti-rent convention on Janury 15 and 16, 1845. Over 200 delegates traveled to Berne to meet in this church. The two days were spent in counting the legislative gains secured by the Anti-Renters and agreeing to support in the future only political candidates favorable to their cause. One important aftermath of this convention was the publication of a weekly anti-rent paper, "The Albany Freeholder".

To prevent the extension in the future of the leasehold system, and to dispose forever of feudal privilege in New York State, the Constitutional Convention of 1846 prohibited leases of land that claimed rent or service, but did not disturb existing leases. The income that landlords derived from their rents was taxed, and the Legislature abolished the right of the landlord to seize the goods of a defaulting tenant. In 1852, the Court of Appeals outlawed the "quarter-sales" and investigations of titles were conducted by the Attorney General. Harassed by all of the above, the Van Rensselaers had sold out their interests by 1850, much of that in the Helderbergs being bought by Colonel Walter Church, a land speculator. A good portion of disputed lands became the property of their owners through purchase, but there was much litigation in the courts for years afterward against speculators who bought up casual or disputed claims.

Stephen Van Rensselaer III (ca. 1812), oil on canvas, 26" x 22¾", Ezra Ames. Courtesy, New York State Historical Association, Cooperstown.

Stephen Van Rensselaer III's life (1764-1839) spanned a period of two distinct cultures. He was born into an aristocratic tradition that contended that men of wealth were pre-ordained to be the leaders of the people in governmental and cultural development. He also lived a great span of his life after the Revolutionary War, under newly developing republican principles that maintained the position that men could achieve their utmost potential regardless of wealth or family position. He was called the *last Patroon* because in 1787 the Legislature had abolished the right of primogeniture - the exclusive right of inheritance belonging to the eldest son.

When Stephen Van Rensselaer III was five years old his father died and his uncle, Abraham Ten Broeck, was appointed guardian of his interests. Stephen was graduated from Harvard in 1782 at the age of 19 and came home to Albany to marry Margaret Schuyler. She was the third daughter of General Philip Schuyler of Revolutionary War fame and the Schuylers were a wealthy landholding family in their own right. In the meantime, his mother, Catherine Livingston Van Rensselaer, daughter of Philip Livingston, a signer of the Declaration of Independence, had married for her second husband the pastor of the First Reformed Dutch Church, the Reverend Eilardus Westerlo. They resided in the Manor House until Stephen's marriage, at which time they removed to the church parsonage.

Upon reaching his majority, Stephen immediately was plunged into the business affairs of managing his manorial legacy. He was the largest landed proprietor in the state. He wanted to bring more of his extensive acreage in the East and West Manors under cultivation and he believed the best way to do this was to continue to lease the land rather than sell. He had much open land in the Helderberg region of Albany County and he advertised this as available for settlement. Many came, from Connecticut in particular, to take up his offer of leases in fee, at a moderate rent, for farms of approximately 120 acres laid out by his surveyor. In his long life, he never changed this policy of administering his lands. His brother-in-law, Alexander Hamilton, who had married Elizabeth Schuyler (Margaret Van Rensselaer's sister), was said to be instrumental in advising the Patroon and even drawing up many of the legal procedures that involved the leaseholds.

Lutheran Church (1836), Berne.

80

As a member of the Federal Party, Stephen III won his first seat in the New York State Assembly in 1789 and twice was elected Lieutenant Governor of the State. He was defeated in his bid for the Governorship in 1801 and again in 1813. He served in the War of 1812 as a Major General of the Militia. In 1810, he had been appointed to a State commission to study the possibilities of a route for a western canal. This was one of his major interests throughout his lifetime, and he was later President of the Canal Commission.

In 1821 he was appointed to the commission to revise the State Constitution. Up to this time none but freeholders had been allowed to vote. The landed interests, such as the Van Rensselaers, Schuylers, Livingstons and others had controlled the government almost exclusively. At the Convention, Van Rensselaer was willing to abandon the property qualifications for voters, but he wanted to limit the privilege to those of character and stability in their residence. His theory was not adopted by the delegates and so he refused to put his name to the new constitution. From 1823-1829, he served the city and county of Albany as a member of the U.S. House of Representatives.

Always interested in agriculture, he became president of a Central Board of Agriculture commissioned by the Legislature. The Board was not long in existence, but he used his own funds to sponsor several extensive geological and agricultural surveys of Albany and Rensselaer Counties. Because of his desire for a place of learning that would advance scientific exploration and train teachers in this field, he founded in 1824 the Rensselaer Institute, largely at his own expense. This school developed into the Rensselaer Polytechnic Institute at Troy, N.Y. In 1824, the Albany Institute, a cultural organization, was formed and Stephen Van Rensselaer III served as its first president. In 1831, he became the chief financier of the Mohawk and Hudson Railroad and was its first president.

Stephen Van Rensselaer III died at the Manor House in Albany in January 1839. His passing ended an era in the life of the citizens of Albany County, especially as it pertained to the tenants of the land.

Van Rensselaer Manor House *(ca. 1844)*, *engraving, Eugene Sintzenich. Courtesy, Albany Institute of History and Art.*

The engraving of the Van Rensselaer Manor House, situated about a half mile from the river bank, was drawn by Eugene Sintzenich (?-1857), a professor of drawing and an artist in Albany from 1844-1848. He was also a landscape and portrait painter and his views of Niagara Falls were well-known and widely popular. The Van Rensselaer Manor House, built in 1765, was taken down in 1892 and reconstructed on the campus of Williams College, Williamstown, Massachusetts, where it served as a fraternity house. It was damaged by fire and subsequently taken down.

Greek Temples in Dutch Towns

Thomas Jefferson was an innovative leader of the classical movement in America. He wanted to introduce the classical designs of antiquity into this country and his State Capitol at Richmond, Virginia, became the first American building modeled directly after an actual ancient edifice. In the Georgian period, there had been some suggestions of classical inspiration, taken from Palladio's work, but no columnar order or temple form was apparent. Jefferson favored using the lines of classical republican Rome in his building plans, because he felt it best suited our new principles of government. It was the architect, Benjamin Latrobe (1764-1820) who first popularized Greek architecture in its simplicity and clarity, and it was not long before even the Roman classicism of Jefferson gave way to the simple grandeur of the Greek.

The application of Greek ideas to building was the outgrowth of a search for something that would exemplify the visions of a young, vigorous country. Americans had a special feeling of kinship with the ancient governments of Greece and Rome, unlike that to the feudal states of Europe. The country was developing into an affluent, intellectual society because of its achievements in agriculture and industry and its people were ready for the acceptance of a new style that came from Athens. By 1830 the Greek Revival style was firmly entrenched in upstate New York. In fact, it became the most popular architectural style ever built in America because it was easily adapted to private as well as impressive public buildings. In this new style, all embellishment disappeared and the simplicity of plain, flat surfaces gave a restrained elegance and dignity to the domestic architecture of Albany County.

On the interior of Greek Revival houses, simplicity of surface usually distinguished the trim. Walls were plastered and painted in flat, bright colors or wallpapered, with a rosette of plaster sometimes placed around the ceiling chandelier. The principal rooms opened into each other and the stairways became very simple, with square or round spindles supporting a plain handrail. Mantel pieces became broad expanses of undecorated slabs of wood or marble, fashioned in the post and lintel style of construction of Greek temples. The houses themselves were built of wood, brick or occasionally of indigenous stone and have an impression of massive stability.

A public building in the Greek-Ionic style is the Court of Appeals at Albany. Designed by Henry Rector (1795?-1878?), an Albany architect, it was erected in 1842 for the use of several state offices, and with its portico of six massive Ionic columns is majestic and impressive. In the central lobby, the rotunda, covered by a brilliantly colored and ornamented dome, exemplified the three orders of Greek architecture - plain Doric columns and capitals of the first floor are surmounted by Ionic carved capitals on the second and ornate Corinthian capitals on the third floor.

Court of Appeals (1842), Albany. Courtesy, New York State Department of Commerce.

The Greek Revival house, in one of its more popular versions, was narrow and deep with its portico facing the street, thus giving the main axis of the house a different direction from the Georgian and Federal styles. The Roff-Godfrey house, built in 1850 and located on Route #9 in the Town of Colonie, has a Greek temple facade with Doric columns supporting a full entablature and a low pitched pediment. Like many of its type, the doorway was placed to one side and had a rectangular transom over the door. Two engaged columns flanked by sidelights surround the door. More monumental houses had a series of several large columns rising the full height of the house, supporting the pedimented portico. There were many variations on this theme.

The Roffs and Godfreys were early settlers in *The Boght*, or bend of the Mohawk, northwest of Cohoes. The land on which this Greek Revival house stands was given to Helena Roff by her father when she married James Henry Godfrey, and they built the Greek section on to the little house that originally stood on the property. The rear section of the house is believed to be over 200 years old and was fashioned in the Dutch style with a basement kitchen, two rooms on the main floor and a sleeping loft. When the Greek Revival section was added in 1850, this became a kitchen.

Roff-Godfrey House (1850), Route #9, Town of Colonie.

In the city of Albany blocks of small houses of uniform design in a simple Greek Revival style began to be erected in the early 19th century. These small city houses were two or three stories high, being two rooms deep and about 25 feet in width. The main floor was raised above the street level with steps leading to the entrance doorway. The houses were quite plain on the exterior, the detail surrounding the entrance doorway being the only adornment. The plain lintels of stone or wood were indicative of the Greek Revival style. The two chief rooms on the main floor were often connected by a wide doorway, so that the rooms could be thrown together for entertaining. The simple staircase was placed to one side near the entrance door. This style of house was typical of the cities of New York, and for the next several decades town houses merely showed further developments of this plan.

Metz House (1840), State Street, Albany.

In the Greek style, the trim became broad and flat and window openings became larger. Sometimes, as in the case of the home of Ashur Morse, owner of the mill on the Basic Creek at South Westerlo, the portico was eliminated in favor of a pedimented end wall, with flat or paneled pilasters instead of columns, and with a flush board facing. The house was built in the 1830's and was the home of the descendents of Ashur and Anna Reynolds Morse for over 100 years.

Ashur Morse House (ca. 1830), South Westerlo.

84

Adams Hotel (1838), Delaware Turnpike, Delmar. Courtesy, Capital District Business Review.

A simple public building in the Greek style is the former Bethlehem Town Hall in Delmar. It was built in 1838 by Nathaniel Adams, to serve as a public lodging house and tavern. Adams had operated the Marble Pillar Refectory at State and Market Streets in Albany. By 1836, he had removed to the country area now encompassed by Delmar, where he conducted his tavern and also farmed the surrounding land.

The restrained detail of Greek Revival houses and public buildings persisted until mid-century. By then, a new wave of population and prosperity brought about by the factory system and the growth of commerce and finance, brought different building ideas to the fore. It would appear that a generation of newly-rich Albanians wanted to show off what they had accomplished. One means of doing this was by the building of ostentatious houses in a totally new style, just as had been done fifty years before with the upsurge of Greek Revival.

General Peter Gansevoort's daughter, Maria (1791-1872), married Allan Melville in 1814. Melville came to Albany from a prosperous mercantile family of Boston, seeking to establish himself in business. After a few years he became disappointed with the dry goods business which he established, and removed his family to New York City where he established a dry goods firm. After many fluctuations in the business world and much borrowing of money from Albany banks and his Gansevoort in-laws, Melville was bankrupt in 1830 and returned to Albany with his family. He bought a fur hat factory, but in striving to get it on a sound financial basis, he overworked, fell ill and died in 1832.

Maria was left with a fashionable home on Clinton Square, two doors from her brother Peter's residence, and eight children ranging in age from two to sixteen. The third of these children was Herman Melville (1819-1891) who would later achieve fame as a writer. He studied at the Albany Academy, but lacking finances for higher education he had no formal studies beyond the age of 15. In 1834, he worked as a clerk for the New York State Bank. At age 17 he went to sea as a cabin boy on a ship bound for Liverpool. He came back in a few months and taught school in Pittsfield and East Albany. Not finding this to his liking, he made a voyage on a whaling ship to the South Seas. He soon began writing about the experiences and composed adventure stories based on the situations and people that he encountered. He is best known for his novel of whale hunting, the celebrated *Moby Dick*, considered by many to be the great American novel.

Melville's early works were written in a firm, classical style filled with observations and adventurous spirit. He was one of America's most imaginative writers and a master of prose. After producing both successes and failures, he became bogged down in writing about moral and philosophical dilemmas that did not appeal to the tastes of the 19th century reader. His ideas were ahead of his time and he was ignored and misunderstood. Melville's ill health and nervous depressions interfered further with his literary attempts and he was forced to take a menial job in the New York Customs House in 1866. His writings were relegated to the back waters of the literary scene until the 20th century, when readers rediscovered his stories.

Melville House (ca. 1829), Albany.

King House Parlor (1839), Albany. Courtesy, Henry Francis duPont Winterthur Museum.

By 1815 Rufus H. King (1794-1867) had come from Connecticut to Albany and was in partnership with his brother-in-law, William McHarg, in a mercantile business. His wholesale dry goods business at 49 State Street was an outgrowth of this and continued for a number of years. By 1840 King became the third president of the New York State Bank, a position he held until his death. In 1861, he was elected to the presidency of the Albany Savings Bank and in 1862 he became president of the Albany Insurance Company. All of these financial enterprises made him an outstanding citizen of Albany, and he built an elaborate house at 1 Park Place in Albany in 1839, near the Albany Academy building.

The parlor of this house illustrates the degree of elegance that could be obtained in the Greek Revival period in the more elaborate mansions. Around the doorway and window openings pillars support classical entablatures and the mantelpiece of Italian marble has carved caryatides supporting the shelf, with a cast iron surround in a fanciful design. Between 1815-1840 the adaptation of classical forms for use in furniture, as well as achitecture, produced what is known as *neo-Greek* or the *Empire* style. The lines of this furniture are symbolized in the *klismos* chair, at the left of the center table, in which the line of the back and seat rail flows gracefully into the incurved legs. The side table near the fireplace shows the architectural flavor given to the furniture of the Empire period with its front legs in the form of marble columns resting on gilded paw feet. Leading designers of the Empire style were found first in Paris and London. The style was brought to New York in 1803 by Charles Honore Lannuier, who made many pieces in the latest French fashion for the Van Rensselaer family.

Cooksburg Inn (first half of 19th century), Cooksburg.

There were five trails or paths used by the Indians through the southwest part of the county leading from the Hudson River, through the valley of the Catskill Creek, to the Schoharie Valley. The Stockbridge and Schoharie tribes frequented these trails in the summer for the purpose of hunting and fishing along the creek, with their camping grounds near the present village of Preston Hollow, in southwestern Albany County.

Route 145 follows a part of these old trails, and beside that road stands the Greek Revival inn at Cooksburg. In earlier times, the road was known as the Loonenburg Turnpike, opened in 1802 from Athens on the Hudson River, and running through Cooksburg, Preston Hollow, Rensselaerville and on to Cherry Valley on the Great Western Turnpike (Route 20). Over the turnpike, droves of sheep and cattle, grain and produce from the interior were taken to the river landings. The inn at Cooksburg served as a stopping place for groups of drovers and farmer guests from Otsego, Delaware and Schoharie counties, going to and returning from market with their produce. The fluted Ionic columns across the front of the inn add a note of elegance to the otherwise simple structure.

A Baptist church was established in 1787 in the village of Preston Hollow, Town of Rensselaerville. This church building was constructed in simple style in 1845 by a local carpenter, Peter Bear, who also built dwellings in the area. His descendents, through the Teter family, are still builders in the local community. The design in the rectangular frieze on the tympanum is found on several houses in the vicinity and indicates their construction by Peter Bear. These decorations were a stock millwork item which could be purchased.

Religion was exciting and dramatic in the 1830's and 40's and revival meetings were an outgrowth of a renewed interest in religion at this period. A new type of church was needed to handle the many people who came to hear the preachers and participate in the revival meetings. The colonial type of church with its box pews was not suited to this and so an auditorium type of church was developed, sometimes having at its front entrance a recessed porch with two Doric columns. There are many Greek Revival type churches in Albany County that were built between 1830-1850.

A well-known innkeeper from Potter Hollow was Potter Palmer (1826-1902). His family were Quakers who came to the Potter Hollow area in the early 1800's from New Bedford, Massachusetts. Benjamin Palmer married Rebecca Potter, whose forebears had settled the village of Potter Hollow in 1806, and for whom it was named. Their son, Potter Palmer began work in dry goods stores in Durham (Greene County) and in Oneida, N.Y. He looked for greater merchandising opportunities and by 1852 visited New York and Chicago to try and decide in which city he would settle. He chose Chicago and there established a dry goods store which he later sold to Marshall Field. By 1870, he had directed his attention to real estate development and in this field, he made one of the large fortunes of this country. He is credited with promoting State Street and its Loop area in Chicago into the busy mercantile center it is today. He also built *The Palmer House*, which is still one of the nation's foremost hotels. Army headquarters in that city led General Philip H. Sheridan, a native Albanian, and his family, to be among the early residents of the Palmer House.

Baptist Church (1845), Preston Hollow.

Titans of the Age

The 19th century appeared to be one of the periods of time in which both men and women seemed to stretch their vigor and capabilities and attained a high point of achievement. The progress in industry, transportation and communication undoubtedly accounted for some of this, as well as an awakening intellectual fervor.

The tireless energy and personal magnetism exhibited by Eliphalet Nott (1773-1866) made him a giant of his time. Born in Connecticut, the grandson and brother of ministers, he also became a pulpit orator of distinction, a leader in the ranks of education, a reformer and philanthropist, as well as a business entrepreneur.

He prepared for college with his brother, Rev. Samuel Nott, earning money for his education by teaching. In 1795, he entered Brown University, and, upon taking a special examination, was granted a degree of Master of Arts in less than a year's time. In 1796, he married Sarah Benedict at Plainfield, Connecticut, daughter of one of his early tutors. By 1796, he decided to settle in New York State and undertook a mission to western New York for his church. Upon riding down into Cherry Valley, he received and took a call to become pastor of the Presbyterian church there. He served two years in the ministry at Cherry Valley, also founding an academy in which he taught. While traveling to a Presbytery meeting at Salem, Washington County, he stopped overnight at an inn in Schenectady. Taking part in a religious service that evening, he so impressed Rev. John Blair Smith with his abilities that he was invited to be a candidate for the pulpit at First Presbyterian Church in Albany.

Assuming that pulpit in 1798, he soon was considered one of America's greatest pulpit orators. He delivered a discourse, at the request of the Albany Common Council, on the occasion of the death of Alexander Hamilton in 1804, considered one of his greatest sermons. In 1804, his wife passed away, leaving him with four children who had to be sent out to live with relatives and friends. He was so distressed by this upheaval that his health became impaired. He felt that he should look for some other position that would be less taxing than the active pastorate of a large city church.

When the presidency of Union College became vacant in 1804, the trustees chose Nott for that post. He was particularly suited for it, as the teaching of youth had always been one of his satisfactions. The college was small and struggling financially but under his leadership it grew rapidly. He introduced a scientific course as an alternative to the strictly classical curriculum then in vogue, making Union a pioneer in this field. He was also active in temperance and abolition work. In 1807, he remarried and brought his family together again.

When Henry Inman painted Eliphalet Nott in 1839, Nott was at the mid-point of his college career. He presided at Union until his death in 1866, a term of 62 years. The excellent full length portrait shows the subject garbed in appropriate academic robes. A portion of Nott's life is detailed by the imposing vista of Union College in the background, which includes Ramee's design of the campus. The Bible, resting on the ledge, signifies his ministerial role.

Eliphalet Nott (1839), oil on canvas, 8' x 5', Henry Inman. Union College Collection.

In addition to his interests in preaching and teaching, by 1815 Eliphalet Nott had made his first stove, experimenting with the properties of heat. In the early 19th century, cast iron box stoves were common but not efficient. Wood, as a source of fuel, was becoming scarce. Soft coal was a dirty fuel and no one had been able to produce a stove that would burn "stone coal", as anthracite was called then. By 1826 Nott had designed the base burner stove, his rotary grate being an innovation. This grate shook down the ash which had previously smothered the fire, so that the burning coals could feed on the draft. Nott financed his own company to produce his stoves. H. Nott and Company was located at Albany in 1827, at the junction of Washington and Central Avenues, under the management of his sons, Howard and Benjamin. They soon became the largest manufacturers of stoves in Albany, contributing to the pre-eminence of the city in stove manufacture in the 19th century.

These inventions and activities led Nott to purchase a steamboat which he converted to burn anthracite coal in its boilers. This venture was a success, but not desiring to pursue it further, he sold out to a rival company, the Hudson River Assn., within a few years. In his lifetime, Eliphalet Nott secured over 30 patents for steam boilers and generators.

Two of his sons, Benjamin and Joel married into the wealthy Cooper family of Albany. In 1843, Benjamin removed from "Normanvale" in Guilderland, to the Town of Bethlehem. His child, Charles DeKay Nott became a Presbyterian minister, ordained in 1859 at the First Reformed Church of Bethlehem at Selkirk, his home church. Another son, John C. Nott, was a prominent Albany County judge. Their mother was a sister of General John Taylor Cooper, a lawyer and officer in the State Militia who maintained a farm at Cedar Hill as well as a residence in Albany.

The painter, Henry Inman (1801-1846), was born in Utica, but in 1812 moved with his parents to New York City. By 1814, he was an apprentice to the portrait painter, John Wesley Jarvis, and assisted him by painting in the backgrounds of canvasses and parts of costumes. In 1822, his apprenticeship ended, he spent a few years in Philadelphia, but the main portion of his life was spent in New York City. When he reached his majority, Inman became a serious painter who did excellent portraits and numerous landscapes and historical subjects. He was considered one of the most prestigious artists of his era.

Nott Stove (ca. 1830), 6' x 3', bearing mark "Nott's Patent". Courtesy, Schenectady Museum Collection.

Erastus Corning (1794-1872) became one of the leading citizens of Albany County during his long and eventful life. At 13 years of age, he moved with his family from Connecticut to Chatham, N.Y., where his father engaged in farming and he attended the common school. His maternal uncle, Benjamin Smith of Troy, apprenticed him as a clerk in his hardware store in 1807. By 1822 Corning had moved to Albany where he soon became a partner in the hardware firm of Spencer and Company, and he continued in this business for over half a century. He took advantage of an opportunity to purchase a small foundry and rolling mill for the making of nails. In these early years he also was forming political opinions that would align him with the Democratic Party.

He soon realized the significance railroads would play in the future development of the country and in 1831 he was one of the promoters of the Mohawk and Hudson River railroad. In 1835, he formed a land company for the purpose of establishing a commercial center at the head of navigation on the Chemung River where the village of Corning was established and named in his honor. From there, a railroad was built connecting the coal fields of Pennsylvania with the Chemung Canal and then with the Erie Canal.

His greatest achievement was the unification, in 1853, of ten small railroad lines to form the New York Central, the largest industrial corporation in America in its time. John V. L. Pruyn, a noted Albany lawyer, aided Corning in this venture. That same year Corning bought 250 acres of the Van Rensselaer estate at West Albany and erected works for making and repairing railroad cars. He put the first sleeping cars on the New York Central in 1858. The St. Marie ship canal was developed under his leadership, aiding in the development of the rich mining interests of Lake Superior. Mr. Corning was a director of the Michigan Central and the Chicago and Burlington railroads, making these lines a connecting link in the great railroad chain. Meanwhile, his Albany Iron Works had developed into a thriving enterprise and produced the rolled plate armor, bars and rivets for the construction of the first iron-clad boat, the *Monitor* of Civil War fame. This, and other iron companies located here, made Albany County one of the country's major iron manufacturing centers in the 19th century.

Active in politics, he was four times Mayor of the City of Albany and also served as a State Senator and Democratic Representative in Congress. He served on the Board of Regents for 39 years, being Vice-Chancellor at the time of his death. In 1833, he had been elected a Vice-President of the New York State Bank, but retired from that position to accept the presidency of the Albany City Bank (later absorbed by the National Commercial Bank), which he retained through life. He was a great community benefactor, especially to schools and churches. With his death in 1872, one of the 19th century magnates, who personified the American Dream, passed from the scene in Albany County. He left a legacy of community service; his grandson Edwin Corning served as Lieutenant Governor of New York under Governor Alfred E. Smith and his great grandson, Erastus Corning II (b. 1909) has served as Mayor of Albany since 1942.

Charles Loring Elliott (1812-1868), who painted the portrait of Erastus Corning, was born in Scipio, N.Y., and died in Albany. As a young man, Elliott worked for a time in the studio of John Trumbull and also studied under John Quidor. He was an itinerant portrait painter in Western New York in the 1830's and opened a studio in New York City in 1840. A natural likeness of the sitter, with clear color and firm drawing were the characteristics of his paintings. He was said to have painted over 700 portraits of famous people, including three New York governors.

Erastus Corning (1864), oil on canvas, 50⅝" x 40⅝", Charles Loring Elliott. Courtesy, Albany Institute of History and Art.

In the early 19th century the village of Rensselaerville was rustically isolated from railways and major highways. It was an agricultural community boasting a grist mill, lumber yard and woolen mill. Francis Conkling Huyck and his father operated the general store in the little village.

About the time of the Civil War it was discovered that paper could be made of wood pulp and this increased enormously the American paper industry. The papermaker's felts, wide woolen bands that carried the wet pulp through the paper machine, were imported from England. Francis Huyck had a headful of ideas, and one of them was that he could make these felts in the old woolen mill in Rensselaerville. In 1870, with a $5000 stake from his father, he went into partnership with Henry Waterbury, who had a technique for joining flat goods to make seamless felts. The next eight years were a time of experiment and struggle. Felts had to be hauled about the countryside for farm wives to do the joining at home; wagons and stage coaches from distant Albany had to haul in raw materials and take out the finished product.

Huyck had his eyes on wider vistas. Within his reach was Albany, linked to the world by ships that lined its waterfront and by the railways crossing the county. He leased a textile plant located on the Normanskill Creek at Kenwood, south of Albany. The felts produced in this mill soon won acclaim as being superior to those produced in Britain. The business expanded rapidly, but on May 4, 1894 disaster struck in the form of fire that burned the Kenwood mills to the ground. Headlines in the Albany Argus newspaper read: "Largest Felt Mill in the United States Succumbs, A Prey to Flames, Hands to the Number of 175 Thrown Out of Work". Immediately Francis Huyck declared that he was full of schemes for building again. He chose to move across the river to Rensselaer to construct his new mill, but the Albany County heritage was carried on in the trade name of "Kenwood". The company continually has expanded its business of making papermaker's felts and synthetic fabrics for paper making machines, under the name of The Huyck Corporation. Its plant in Rensselaer is one of several branches that are located chiefly in the southern United States. There are also branches of the company in Canada, England, South America and Japan.

Huyck Store Poster (19th century), Rensselaerville. Courtesy, New York State Library.

Albany County achieved fame in the sphere of natural sciences because of several well-known personages who moved here.

James Hall (1811-1898) was graduated from Rensselaer Polytechnic Institute in 1832. While studying there, he was influenced greatly by Professor Amos Eaton, who had a capacity for arousing enthusiasm for the natural sciences in his young students. James Hall proved to be an apt pupil. After graduation, he spent the summer studying the geology of the Helderberg mountains. Eaton brought him to the attention of "the Albany Patroon", Stephen Van Rensselaer III, through whom he was appointed to assist in a geological survey of the state. After completion of his portion of this work, and because of his excellent reports, Hall was commissioned to prepare a report on the paleontology of the state, which occupied him for over 50 years. In 1866 he was appointed Director of the New York State Museum, which became a repository for much of his great collections of fossils and minerals. In 1893, he was named State Geologist, a position created especially for him. His works received world-wide recognition in scientific circles because of their scope.

The brick building which James Hall erected in 1856 served for over 50 years as his office and laboratory. It was an influential center of geological science in this country. Here he gathered about himself men who later achieved distinction in geology in many parts of the world. The building now houses the Sunshine School facility in Lincoln Park, Albany.

James Hall's Office and Laboratory (1856), Albany. Courtesy Morris Gerber Collection.

Coach House - Jermain Estate (19th century), Menands.

James Barclay Jermain (1809-1897) was a noted philanthropist, born in Albany, the son of Sylvanus Jermain, a commission merchant who accumulated a large fortune. A director of the Mechanics and Farmers Bank, James Jermain was admitted to practice in the Supreme Court of New York State in 1836. He dispensed his fortune wisely and among his many projects was the endowment of a professorship at Williams College, the establishment of the Jermain Memorial Presbyterian Church in Menands, a children's home in Watervliet and the YMCA building on North Pearl Street in Albany, as well as an Old Men's Home in Menands.

The Jermain family resided at *Hedge Lawn*, an estate located between Albany and Watervliet. Sylvanus Jermain had purchased the house from General William Jenkins Worth, a distinguished soldier in the War of 1812 and the Mexican War, who lived there when not in active service to his country. James Jermain brought his bride to Hedge Lawn in 1843 and he resided there until his death.

Interior at Arbour Hill (1878), oil on canvas, 25" x 20", Walter Launt Palmer. Courtesy, Albany Institute of History and Art.

Thomas Worth Olcott was born in Hudson, N.Y., and educated in the schools there. He began a financial career as a clerk in the Columbia Bank of Hudson, where he was employed two years. He had an alert mind for financial matters and when the Mechanics and Farmers Bank of Albany opened in July of 1811 he came there as one of the clerical staff. Within six years he was named Cashier and in 1836 he was elected President, which position he occupied for 44 years. A great share of the success of this bank should be credited to the financial genius of Thomas W. Olcott. This was the third bank incorporated in Albany and was chartered for the benefit of the mechanics and farmers of Albany County and originally its charter stated that none but these should be elected as bank officers. Up to this time, the ownership or management of Albany banks had been centered in small groups of prominent business men and the monied upper class.

Mr. Olcott was not only considered the outstanding banker of Albany, but he was philanthropic and civic-minded as well. He was vice-president and later president of the first board of directors of the Albany Law School, organized in 1851, and the fourth school of its kind in the United States. He served on many boards, the more prominent being the Dudley Observatory, Albany Hospital, Albany Academy and the Albany Cemetery Association. He was also president of the Albany and West Stockbridge Railroad, which later merged with the Boston and Albany. He gave assistance to the government on perfecting plans for a national bank system and in 1863 declined an offer from President Lincoln to become First Comptroller of the Currency.

In 1855 the Mechanics and Farmers Savings Bank was incorporated. This was a savings bank and had no relationship to the Mechanics and Farmers Bank, which was a commercial lending institution. Thomas W. Olcott was the first president of the Mechanics and Farmers Savings Bank and was succeeded by his son, Dudley. This connection of the Olcotts, father and son, covered more than a full century of banking interests.

Thomas W. Olcott was painted sitting in the parlor of his home "Arbour Hill" (Ten Broeck Mansion) in 1876 by Walter Launt Palmer (1856-1932), the son of sculptor Erastus Dow Palmer. Walter Launt Palmer was a talented Albany artist who became well-known, especially for his paintings of snow scenes in the late 19th century. His several paintings of Albany interiors give us a valuable historical document of the period in which they were painted.

Purveyors of the News

A great increase in reading of newspapers and periodicals was brought about in the 19th century by the growth of popular education and interest in public affairs. Advances in printing techniques also helped the circulation of newspapers to increase with each passing year.

Newspapers had been published in Albany from 1771, but the first one of lasting importance was the *Albany Argus*, published in 1813 by Jesse Buel (1778-1839). After a successful newspaper career, Buel turned to agriculture and published *The Cultivator* in 1834 under the auspices of the State Agricultural Society, formed in Albany in 1832 to promote and encourage agriculture. By 1866 that paper had been merged with *The Country Gentleman*, founded by Luther Tucker in Albany in 1853 and published in Albany until recent times.

Thurlow Weed (1797-1882), one of the greatest political journalists of any age, came to Albany in 1815 to work at the *Argus*. In his long career as a political boss, he aided William Seward in political ventures as well as helped secure the Presidential nominations for Harrison, Clay and Taylor. In Albany, Weed founded *The Evening Journal* which was published from 1830 to 1862 and was a Whig Party paper that later became one of the leading vehicles of the Republican Party in New York State, in which Weed was very influential. It was through his journalistic influences that he accomplished many of his political feats.

Another newspaperman of note in Albany was Solomon Southwick (1773-1839), who managed *The Albany Register* in the early part of the 19th century. In 1819 he established *The Ploughboy*, an agricultural paper. In his career he also held many political positions, but was defeated for the governorship by Martin Van Buren.

Joel Munsell (1808-1880) was one of Albany's most influential citizens, being the foremost printer in this area. His accomplishments included author, publisher, book seller and historian. He collected, compiled and edited collections of historical material, family histories and genealogies. He also printed catalogs for many of Albany's business and industrial concerns as well as circulars, hand bills, cards and programs. He preserved much of Albany's history in his ten volume *Annals of Albany*, published in the 1850's, and was a founder of the Albany Institute, one of the parent organizations of the present Albany Institute of History and Art.

The silhouette of Joel Munsell, although unsigned, is similar in style to the work of William H. Brown. The silhouette is pasted on a lithographic background and Munsell is standing on Jefferson Street, Albany, with the state capitol building in the background.

Thurlow Weed, oil on canvas, 35" x 30", Asa Twitchell. Courtesy, New York Historical Association, Cooperstown.

Silhouette of Joel Munsell. Courtesy, Albany Institute of History and Art.

Albany Basin *(ca. 1850)*, engraving by Hatch and Severyn after a drawing by John William Hill. Courtesy, New-York Historical Society, New York City.

After 1800, with the rise of book and magazine publishing that centered here, landscape engravings became one of the subjects of interest in these publications. The groundwork for later romantic landscape painting was laid by the painters who produced views of American cities, country estates, farm animals, etc., for reproduction as aquatint engravings, etchings and woodcuts, as illustrations for newspapers and periodicals. The engraving of *The Albany Basin* was done about 1850 by the firm of Hatch and Severin of New York, after a drawing by John William Hill (1812-1879). The twin-spired Cathedral of the Immaculate Conception dominates the skyline at the top of Madison Avenue on the left center of the picture. This church was built in 1852 from a design by Patrick Keeley of New York City, who came to the United States from Ireland in 1841. Over 500 Catholic Churches in upstate New York were built from his plans. The Cathedral is patterned after the Cathedral of Cologne, Germany, and is the seat of the Catholic Diocese of Albany. Prominent engraving companies in Albany were Rawdon and Clark, working from 1826, and Gavit and Company from 1859. John E. Gavit was one of the founders of The American Bank Note Company in New York.

A Passing Fancy - Victorianism in Architecture

By mid-century, a period of confusing eclecticism in architecture, rich in the motifs of the past, was beginning to be seen in the succession of styles derived from historical sources. Education and travel had produced in Americans a growth of historical knowledge. There was a desire to return to the romantic days of the Middle Ages for architectural inspiration and the Gothic Revival became a re-adaptation of the medieval forms of the past. Albany County houses of the 17th century had been derived directly from medieval Gothic styles of northern Europe, and the "new" Gothic was a decorative form of this style. There was a new feeling of attention to the natural landscape, as opposed to the formal garden of colonial times. The desire was to incorporate the house to fit its environment, in an attempt to combine rural architecture and rural scenery.

The residence of Joel T. Rathbone (1806-1863) was called by A. J. Downing, "one of the finest specimens of Gothic or Pointed style of architecture in this country."[5] Andrew Jackson Downing (1815-1852) was one of America's foremost landscape gardeners and he planned the grounds of the Rathbone estate. While Downing's chief interest was landscape, he also drafted models for houses in the Gothic style as well as complete lists of plants and trees to be used in their landscaping. Downing stressed the relationship between house and site and the need to create a setting for beauty's own sake.

The house itself was built from the plans of Alexander J. Davis (1803-1892), in 1849. Davis was one of the most successful architects of his generation. He, like Downing, was a dedicated romantic, true to the flavor of his time, and he was also an excellent draftsman. He realized that not everyone could afford personal architectural supervision and he published books of house patterns that could be executed by local builders anywhere in the country.

Rathbone's estate covered 120 acres of wooded hillside, just south of Albany, with a view of the Hudson River. The house was designed in a Tudor style and represented a great degree of elegance. The main floor was centered by a graceful 16-foot circular hall, from which radiated the drawing room, dining room and library, as well as a sleeping chamber, staircase hall and office. The second floor sleeping apartments contained six bedrooms with baths, and servant's quarters were located on the third floor. Large additions were made to the house after it was erected to make it even more spacious than in the original plan.

In 1858, the Rathbone property was sold to the Catholic Diocese to serve as the home of the Convent and Academy of the Sacred Heart. A portion of the Rathbone mansion was incorporated into the new buildings that were erected to house the novitiate. The gatehouse of the original estate, as well as the carriage house and a superintendent's cottage, still remain on the grounds.

"Architectural Drawing - Projected design for Kenwood, South Albany, A.J. Davis", (1849). Courtesy, Metropolitan Museum of Art, Harris Brisbane Dick Fund, 1924.

John Ruskin was influencing popular thought by his studies of art and sociological research. He denounced the materialism of the age and urged a return to the ecclesiasticism of the Middle Ages. His works were read widely by the American middle class who translated his ideas into Gothic houses of wood and stucco, with steep roofs and arches, traceried eaves and latticed windows. The jig saw could cut out fanciful shapes for barge boards and railings. Machines provided cheap lumber and millwork for the new styles, but spelled the downfall of the hand craftsmanship of earlier times.

Doorway of Paddock-Brezee House, Preston Hollow.

Schoolcraft House (1835), Route #20, Guilderland.

John Schoolcraft was Superintendent of the Albany Glass Works at Guilderland and in 1835 he erected a *Carpenter Gothic* style home beside the Great Western Turnpike (Route #20) in Guilderland. The house is somewhat reminiscent of the pointed Tudor style of A. J. Downing with diamond paned windows and drip hood molds, cut out crested railing on the roof and bay and the wooden tower suggestive of crenelations. The barge board motif has lobes with trefoil bosses at the points and the heavy ornate wooden finials and Gothic tracery above the bay add a medieval flavor to the house. The siding is flushboard rather than the earlier clapboard of the colonial style house. In the Gothic style of architecture, towers, gables, dormers, clustered chimneys and bay windows all helped to give prominence to the surface rather than to the mass of the house.

Broad, plain surfaces were considered monotonous in the Gothic era and thus wide boards covered with a narrow strip at the place of joining gave a varied texture to the sides of the cottage built near Rensselaerville by G. W. Durant, the headmaster of the Rensselaerville Academy. In a letter of December 2, 1854, he mentions that he has built his home "similar to a house built in the village of Cooperstown". This *board and batten* technique can also be found on sheds and small barns built in the 19th century.

In the Gothic era, white paint, which was popular in the Federal and Greek styles, was replaced for house colors with a mellow faun or gray and the house details often were painted in darker shades of the same colors. This color scheme was thought to bring the house into harmony with the natural surroundings. In the interiors, the houses exhibited a high narrowness, with heavy dark woodwork and fireplaces covered with slabs of marble, while bracketed, arched and domed forms were used both inside and out.

Durant House (ca. 1854), Rensselaerville.

Learned House (1873), State Street, Albany.

The Gothic form of architecture advocated by the Englishman, John Ruskin, is quite apparent in the William L. Learned house at 298 State Street, Albany. Built in 1873, the house is a Ruskinian late Gothic house of brick, notable for its horizontal bandings and patterns of alternating colors and materials in the arches over the windows and its shaped lintels. There is an ecclesiastical feeling to the columns and arched opening over the front entranceway. William Learned was a justice of the Supreme Court of New York.

The period of great financial and industrial growth before and after the Civil War brought about a surge of building that produced many diverse ideas about architectural styles. Also, changes in the cultural life of the people brought forth new ideas about the equality of man and the freedom of choice. People desired a house that was a personal expression - one that would be different from that of one's neighbor.

One of the expressions for a different type of dwelling was the Italian Renaissance *palazzo* style, which was the most popular urban style of the mid-century. The Chauncey Pratt Williams house at 284 State Street, Albany, was built in 1860. It is a six-bay wide Italianate brownstone with a recessed central bay and rich ornamentation. Williams was one of Albany's "lumber barons" and the C. P. Williams and Company were lumber dealers.

Williams House (1860), State Street, Albany.

Baker House (ca. 1870), Cedar Hill.

By 1870 the Italian style, derived from the Renaissance villas of Italy, had spread to the rural sections. Many of these houses had a low pyramidal roof with pavilions with roofs at different levels that made them irregular in mass and picturesque in style. Often there was an asymetrically placed tower, in imitation of the *campanile* or bell tower. Originally built as sprawling stone estates for the wealthy, the style soon was adapted to wood and simplified for the average family. A villa in the Italianate manner was the country home of Cornelius V. Baker, known as Grand View Farm, which overlooks the Hudson River at Cedar Hill. In 1846, Mr. Baker married Caroline Lasher and settled on a part of the Nicoll-Sill tract, purchasing 120 acres. Subsequently, he enlarged his holding to 450 acres and the farm became one of the most productive in Albany County. The Baker farm was renowned for its excellent melons, which were grown on the river flatlands and shipped to markets here and abroad. The original house was enlarged and renovated over the years until it reached its present state of development in the 1870's.

The Archibald Greene house, built in 1872 at Westerlo, is another variation of the Italianate style. Greene was a prosperous dealer in general merchandise and his house is one of the most elaborate homes in Westerlo. It has a symmetrical five-bay facade with fancy bracketed eaves and a center pedimented pavilion having a third story garret window above the entrance. The kitchen-utility wing at the right of the structure complements the main house.

Greene House (1872), Westerlo.

The pylons and gateways to Egyptian temples and tombs served as the pattern for Egyptian Revival architecture in America. The receiving vault at the Albany Rural Cemetery in Menands was built in 1858 by John Bridgford at a cost of $5,358., after a design by Woolett. A second vault was built in 1883 in the same style as the first one. The flat roof line, smooth monolithic exterior and tall straight-headed entranceway give a monumental effect that was found particularly suitable for cemetery entrance gateways and vault structures. Also, springing up on the American landscape at this period were Oriental, Tudor, Flemish, castellated, Moorish and Swiss Chalet types of dwellings, all adding to the diversity of the age.

Receiving Vaults - Albany Rural Cemetery (1858-1883), Menands.

Robert Johnston House (1874), Cohoes. Occupied by 3 generations of managers of Harmony Mills.

After the middle of the century, French Renaissance designs came into popularity with the desire to emulate the styles of the Second Empire of Napolean III, as seen in the buildings of Paris. This school of French architecture was based on classic rather than Gothic principles of architecture. Tall mansard or curb roofs, added above a bracketed cornice, gave an imposing quality to simple structures and added more height to the upper story rooms. A cupola was one of the marks of distinction, and ceilings, windows and doors became excessively high, adding to the tall narrowness of rooms and halls.

George N. Best (d. 1917) made a fortune from cutting Hudson River ice and shipping it to New York City. About 1884 he built this palatial mansard roof mansion along the river shores at Cedar Hill, about six miles below Albany. The land on which this house stands was conveyed by Stephen Van Rensselaer II, the seventh Lord of the Manor, to Adam Winne, by indenture of lease in perpetuity on September 1, 1769, as stated in a legal search of the property. Barent S. Winne owned the land in 1857 and it progressed through several owners to George N. Best in 1884. In 1912, Best deeded to the Knickerbocker Ice Company of New York City "all the right to cut ice in the Hudson River in front of all lands... on the west bank of the said river, lying north and south of the ice house."[6]

Best House (1884), Cedar Hill.

By the 1880's, the Queen Anne and Shingle styles had evolved, which imitated loosely the forms of English architecture of the 17th and 18th centuries. There were picturesque details such as half timbering, turrets and bay windows and patterned shingle work. The interiors had become dark and rich, with many textures and an accumulation of possessions displayed on a profusion of shelves and niches. Interior planning, however, had become much less rigid and there was increasingly a free handling of the flow of interior space.

Executive Mansion (ca. 1850), Eagle Street, Albany, Courtesy, New York State Department of Commerce.

The Executive Mansion in Albany exhibits many of the characteristics of the Queen Anne style with its clustered chimneys, turrets, gables, porches and *porte-cochere*, as well as a tower. The original part of the dwelling was owned by Thomas Olcott in the 1850's and leased to the State in 1874 to serve as the residence of Governor Samuel Tilden. The State bought the house for use as the Executive Mansion in 1877 and many additions and renovations were made at that time and in the ensuing years. This same style of house was duplicated in lesser size, in brick and in wood, throughout various sections of the County in the late 19th century.

George L. Stedman bought a house and 25 acres from Dr. Alden March in 1868. Dr. March and Dr. James Armsby had founded the Albany Medical College in 1838. Stedman winterized Dr. March's summer house and in 1880 built on the same property the shingle house at 410 Loudonville Road. The builder was Richard Wickham, a well known builder in Albany who began his business in this city in 1860. Wickham had a large establishment on Broadway where he built everything needed for his contruction business and employed as many as 130 men. He built public and private houses in New York and adjoining states as well as parts of the Grand Union Hotel at Saratoga Springs, and several other hotels and churches. Two wings were added to the shingle house in 1884 which were incorporated into the original structure by an all-encompassing roof that flows out over the porch, pulling it within the main body of the building. This Americanized version of the Queen Anne style also appears in cottages at Newport, Rhode Island, designed by H. H. Richardson.

Stedman House (1880), Route #9, Loudonville.

An interesting copper weathervane in the form of a dragon was situated atop a carriage house formerly on the grounds of the Vincentian Institute on Madison Avenue in Albany. This carriage house had been a part of the estate of George Hawley, a gentleman who had extensive brewery and other business interests in Albany during the latter part of the 19th century. The vane was eventually sold by the Parish Council and its present whereabouts is unknown. These later vanes were often not used as utilitarian objects, but added visual interest to coach houses and other outbuildings.

Weathervane (late 19th century), Vincentian Institute, Madison Avenue, Albany. Courtesy, Bureau of Historical Services, City of Albany.

At the time of the Gothic Revival in church buildings in America, there was a certain feeling that this style was more "Christian", since Gothic architecture had been used in the great cathedrals of Europe, whereas Greek forms spoke of temples of a pagan civilization. English Gothic became the standard for ecclesiastical structures, especially for Episcopal churches, in the last half of the 19th century.

This echo of the Middle Ages was brought to church architecture by Richard Upjohn (1802-1878) of New York City, designer of St. Peter's Episcopal Church on State Street in Albany, built in 1859. In the design of St. Peter's, there is profuse tracery on the interior and angularity to the capitals, as well as Gothic windows and mosaic pavement. Outside, the various areas are marked off in horizontal lines as though the building was conceived in elevation rather than mass, and there are many three dimensional elements such as buttresses and porches. It was built of Schenectady blue-stone and New Jersey sandstone.

Upjohn's church structures were built in the old tradition of English perpendicular Gothic and were rich and correct to tradition in their use of detail. He wanted his churches to be cathedral-like in feeling and to set a tone of solemnity for the act of worship. His personal feelings of conscientiousness and humility also led him to build many small country churches in wooden board and batten construction that were architecturally pleasing in their own right, and for which he sometimes charged no monetary commission. In 1852, he published a book of "Rural Architecture". The design book was for use in the building of country churches of moderate cost, designed for wood construction, although the treatment became popular for all kinds of buildings that were unpretentious in style.

The work of Richard Upjohn was popular and many commissions, not only for churches, but also residences, flowed into his office. One of these was for alterations to the Manor House of the Van Rensselaers in North Albany, which he renovated in 1840-44. The mansion was remodeled in an adaptation of English Baroque, although the house originally had been English Georgian in style. The wings were remodeled, a front porch added, specific form given to the dormers and New Jersey brown sandstone was adopted as the facing material for trim and foundation. The brick body of the house was painted to harmonize with the trim. This house also had received additions planned by Philip Hooker about 1816. Hooker added the wings to each side of the central block of the house and placed a *piazza* across the rear.

Steeple of St. Peter's Episcopal Church *(1876)*, *watercolor on paper, 24⅞" x 19⅛", Edwin Austin Abbey. Courtesy, Albany Institute of History and Art.*

Edwin Austin Abbey (1852-1911) painted the steeple of St. Peter's Church in watercolor. He was an historical and mural painter, as well as an illustrator, who painted in the traditional academic manner. His black and white drawings with delicate and complicated lines were done for Harper's and Scribner's magazines as well as for many other publications. Abbey was interested in portraying 17th and 18th century England in his illustrations. He was also a painter in oils and watercolors and lived in Philadelphia and New York, but in later life resided in London. He was a friend of William H. Low and Walter Launt Palmer, both Albany artists.

In the 1870's and 80's, Henry Hobson Richardson's (1838-1886) creative architectural genius was recognized in the Romanesque Revival style which he popularized in houses and public buildings. Richardson was a romanticist of great taste and discernment, and he felt that in the elemental 12th century French Romanesque there was a suitability to the American environment. He insisted upon using only the finest material and workmanship in construction and decoration. His public buildings created an impression of massive solidity, with high roofs, clustered windows, deeply arched doors and square or circular towers. His Albany City Hall and Courtroom at the Court of Appeals are two examples of his ability to raise the standard of architectural excellence in the 19th century. The whirling linearity of the carved work at the Court of Appeals chamber was a fore-runner of what was to come in the Art Nouveau period. Richardson's competition drawings of 1883 for the Albany Episcopal Cathedral project were not accepted, but the design is well known in architectural circles.

The western stairway, of Richardson's design, was begun in 1884, but upon his death it was completed by Isaac G. Perry. Its bold naturalistic carving is more Gothic than Renaissance in feeling and was not shown in Richardson's drawings. Hundreds of men labored for a score of years on these carvings, and others within the Capitol.

New York State Capitol (1867), Albany. Courtesy, New York State Department of Commerce.

The New York State Capitol was begun in 1867 by Thomas Fuller. By 1875, so much had been expended over budget, with only two storys completed, that Fuller was fired and it was decided to seek an advisory commission to give an opinion about completing the building. In 1876, Leopold Eidlitz, Frederick L. Olmstead and H. H. Richardson were commissioned to finish the building. The final style became partly Romanesque, partly French Renaissance, with the entire effect one of massive ruggedness.

Western (Million-Dollar) Stairway, New York State Capitol, Albany. Courtesy, New York State Department of Commerce.

The Senate Chamber of the Capitol, designed by Richardson in 1878, is rich and vigorous in detail and the most lavish work of architecture that Richardson ever executed. The materials used in its construction were elegant. Polished panels of Mexican onyx framed with Siena marble, embossed gilded leather, polished columns of red-brown Scottish granite supporting the gallery arches, settee backs of mahogany and leather, and a heavy beamed ceiling of brown carved oak gave rich and varied coloring to the interior. The Chamber was restored to its original appearance in 1978. The stonework was cleaned, the carpet was duplicated in the original pattern and wall surfaces of gilt and leather were replaced. The original gas chandeliers were reproduced and electrified and in the future the original furnishing of the room will be duplicated. The main lobby in front of the Senate Chamber also was restored to its original appearance.

Senate Chamber, New York State Capitol (1878), Albany. Courtesy, Senate Chamber Restoration Press Kit.

The Grange Sard Jr. house at 397 State Street in Albany was commissioned in 1882 and exemplifies the increasing simplicity and restraint of Richardson's later work, and is the first of his buildings to have the masonry arranged in broad and narrow courses, rather than the random ashlar. The house is typical of his work in its massive form and corner tower, its semi-circular arched entranceway and polygonal dormer. The residence faced Washington Park, which was developing rapidly in the 1880's. Sard was a partner in Rathbone and Sard, stove manufacturers of Albany.

Richardson's courtroom, now located in the rear of the Court of Appeals building, is considered to be one of his finest rooms. The courtroom was designed by H. H. Richardson and built in the Capitol in 1884. The room was taken apart and re-erected in the Court of Appeals building in 1917. All of the oak trim, the portraits, the fireplace of Mexican Onyx, the hand-carved oak benches and railings, add to the beauty of the room, although this is a much later addition to the Greek style courthouse of 1842.

Richardson strove to be fresh and individual in his style, while using various traditional elements in a functional design of great power. In his seven story Marshall Field Building in Chicago, with the use of great arcades and expanses of glass, he seems to have perceived the idea of the skeletal design that would produce the skyscraper. It was a utilitarian building stripped of all ornamentation and it greatly influenced modern commercial architecture. Richardson's emphasis on *function* was an idea that would be more fully realized in the 20th century.

Sard House (1882), State Street, Albany.

Squire Whipple (1808-1888) was one of the first civil engineers to develop the theory of stresses in bridge truss designs and one of the men most influential in introducing the age of structural iron to the United States. After being graduated from Union College in 1830, he pursued a career of engineering, residing in Utica and, after 1850, in Albany at 227 State Street. Whipple's first bridge, the cast and wrought-iron bow string truss, was built across a section of the enlarged Erie Canal in the early 1840's and soon became the standard vehicular bridge which was adopted for small local crossings of the Canal. It was the first attempt to use iron as the principal material in bridge construction and Whipple's patented design was so successful that hundreds like it were soon constructed throughout the northeast. Of those built in New York State, the Normanskill bridge is one of only a few that have survived. As late as 1869, Whipple continued to invent new types of lift and draw bridges.

Whipple trusses were pre-fabricated in small sections and assembled on the site. The sections of the chords did not require welding or riveting. They were fitted together with locating pins and held in place by compression when the vertical rods and the wrought iron bowstring links were tightened. The bridges were inexpensive, light in weight, strong and durable and adaptable to a variety of situations. When the Erie Canal was again enlarged in the late 19th century, these Whipple crossing bridges were sold and moved to new locations because they were disassembled easily.

In 1867 a builder of Whipple-type bridges, Simon DeGraff of Syracuse, constructed the bridge that is now at Normanskill Farm, Albany. The original location of the bridge is unknown. When the Albany and Delaware Turnpike (Delaware Avenue) was re-routed in 1899, the Farm bought the 113-foot bridge and re-erected the structure over the deep ravine separating the farm from the roadway.

Whipple Truss Bridge (1867), Albany. Courtesy, Jack Boucher, Historic American Buildings Survey.

By 1874 the growth and prosperity of Cohoes created a demand among its citizens for a repertory theater that would match those springing up in nearby Albany. At this time, acting and the theater arts were in a period of expansive growth nationally. Travelling road shows brought entertainment to people who lived beyond the larger cities.

This new demand for entertainment resulted in the building of the Cohoes Music Hall, an elegant little theater designed by Nichols and Halcott of Albany. The first two floors were designed to house stores and offices, while the Music Hall itself was located on the third floor. The first play presented was *London Assurance* by J. W. Albaugh's Albany company, one of many that brought drama, vaudeville performances and singing programs to the Hall. Appearing on the stage were such notables as James J. Corbett, Eva Tanguey, a native of Cohoes, and Buffalo Bill Cody with a band of Sioux Indians.

After a few years, poor attendance and too many competing theaters doomed the project to failure. The Music Hall was closed, to lie asleep for over seventy years. It now is restored and re-opened to provide theatrical entertainment.

Cohoes Music Hall (1874), Cohoes.

The Halls of Academe

In 1782 Governor George Clinton had urged the Legislature to establish schools for public instruction, and two years later the Board of Regents was formed for that purpose. In 1789 the Legislature set aside unsold lots in each township that could be used for educational purposes. The New England settlers who came in to New York after the Revolution had known the benefits of a common school system and were eager to have public education for their children. Many towns in the post-colonial period had begun to build one room schools on the public lots. A system of school districts for each township was set up by the Legislature in 1812 and the basic educational provision required a common school fund that should be apportioned among the towns. Even with these provisions, school was not compulsory and many children worked to contribute to family support, until child labor laws came into effect.

During the early years of the 19th century there was a growing concern and desire for cultural and educational growth. Friends of education were constantly urging the Legislature to upgrade standards of teaching, and in 1827 New York was the first state to appropriate money to train teachers in academies. By 1844, these institutions had failed to produce enough teachers to meet the need, and the first normal school was established at Albany.

A one-room schoolhouse that has been preserved is that of District #6, Route #146, Guilderland Center, N.Y. Cobblestone buildings were a popular style of construction between 1825-65. Possibly they were built by masons who worked on the Erie Canal. Carved in one of the quoins of this school is "R. E. Zeh, mason, 1860".

A small amount of state money had been set aside for the use of *academies*, which taught classical studies as a college preparatory course to enrolled students. Private enterprise in the 19th century, however, was mainly responsible for the founding of more academies in New York than elsewhere. These academies were private schools that required a tuition payment. The Knoxville Academy at Knox, was considered one of the finest educational institutions in Albany County when it was chartered in 1837. It prepared students for college entrance, as well as to enter teaching or business. There were also academies at Rensselaerville, Coeymans and Preston Hollow, as well as within the cities of Albany and Cohoes. After 1855, the academies began to decline, challenged by the rise of the free public high school.

In 1873 the *Acton Civill Polytechnic Institute* was built on Westerlo Street in Coeymans, to serve as a private school. This building never opened its doors to students, and in 1899 it was bought by District #1 to serve as a grade and high school. The building is now the home of the Coeymans Civic Center. Its Second Empire style is apparent in the mansard roof with straight sides, the porthole dormer and metal cresting on the tower and its classical moldings and details.

Acton Civill Polytechnic Institute (1873), Coeymans.

District #6 School House (1860), Guilderland Center.

Summer at the Boarding House and On The River

The Helderberg hills, with elevations of 1600 feet, offered nature's own air-conditioning to offset the summer's heavy, humid air of the Hudson Valley. After the Civil War, summer vacations to the hill country began to be a special enjoyment for a limited number of people.

City folk took the local train at Albany and disembarked at Meadowdale or Altamont railway stations. There, they were met by *stages* sent down from the boarding houses to convey them and their heavy trunks to the resorts on the escarpment. Mostly, they sat on the wide verandahs and rocked away a week or two, enjoying nature's beauty, the fresh country air and farm style home-cooked meals. The cost of room and board for a week was six to eight dollars. The younger people would hike, swim or boat in the stream or lake and play croquet on the lawn. Once a week all who were able would walk down to the Indian Ladder to sightsee, returning to the boarding house late in the afternoon, hot and dusty from their outing. In the evenings, group singing around the piano, parlor games or dancing would be the diversions.

The White Sulphur Springs Hotel at Berne was built in the early 1870's by Jacob Hochstrasser, Jr., and was named for a mineral spring adjacent to the boarding house. This and other hotels were constructed in a simple manner with the emphasis not on style but upon the number to be accommodated. Most boarders came from Albany or Troy, though one lady visited the Hochstrassers from the Bahamas. She urged them to advertise in Bahamian newspapers for guests, and others from that far away place came to the Helderbergs to spend their summers. People also saw the advertisements in New York City newspapers and took the train to Albany County, for a cool mountain vacation. There were other boarding houses at East Berne and nearby Warner's and Thompson's Lakes. Farmers in the region of the lakes also opened their homes to summer boarders for a time. After World War I, with the advent of the automobile, the boarding house type of vacation went into decline, as people began travelling farther afield.

Beeren (Bear's Island) or Barren Island, as it is locally called, lies just off the Hudson River shoreline at the village of Coeymans, and at one time was a navigable island on both sides. On the west it now has been connected to the mainland with sand dredged from the river. The Patroon had a fort and a number of cannon on the island in 1643 so that he could command the river at the southern entrance to Rensselaerswyck.

In 1879 John N. Briggs purchased the northern part of the island and built a resort for excursion parties that came there by boat, mainly from Albany. He named the resort *Baerena Park* and constructed a large covered dance floor and an observation tower as well as walkways and picnic areas. The excursion parties were mainly church and fraternal groups that came in large hay barges towed by tugs. These excursions ceased in the early 20th century, as newer forms of entertainment enticed people.

Spring House, White Sulphur Springs Hotel (ca. 1870), Berne.

The barges pictured are the *Chicago, Baldwin, Empress* and *Harvest Queen*. The steam launch *Greta* is in the foreground. This little boat conveyed local people from the village of Coeymans to the island. Across the river is the icehouse of Whitbeck and Miller. There were several of these ice houses lining the shores of the river in Albany County. Ice was cut from the river in winter, stored in the vast icehouses until summer, then placed in barges and sent to New York City to supply the homes, hotels and restaurants.

Hudson River Barges (19th century), Coeymans.

Steamboat Albany *(1883), oil on canvas, 57⅞" x 33⅞", Antonio Jacobsen. Courtesy, Albany Institute of History and Art.*

The steamboat *Albany*, painted by Antonio Jacobsen in 1883, was built for the Day Line's Albany to New York service in 1880. It boasted the new innovation of an iron hull rather than the usual wooden hull and had her boilers in the hold, which permitted more deck space. Also, the dining room was placed on the main deck, which was another first. The *Albany* was active in service through 1930, when she then became the *Potomac*, an excursion boat on that river until 1948.

The lure of speed gave birth to the steamboat, and it was not long before those vessels had made obsolete the old passenger sailing packets. Steamboats were improved and enlarged until they became virtual floating palaces of luxurious accommodations for 600 to 800 people. The steamboats excited the imagination of a romantic people and most of them were immortalized in paintings done with accurate detail and bright colors by many artists.

Art for Adornment

Before mid-century, the classical tradition in art was to become as obsolete as the straight lines and plain surfaces of the Greek Revival in architecture. The rapid rise of industrialism and a dramatic rise in population changed the face of the country and influenced a new element in the art world — a surge of romantic painting. By 1840, Americans were preoccupied with the theme of the worth of the common man and his relation to nature and its beauty. The new middle class, made well-to-do by the Industrial Revolution, were eager to adorn the walls of their new homes with beautiful pictures. They preferred scenes of tranquil beauty that were easily understood and pleasant to look at. As huge factories and tenement dwellings scarred the landscape, people returned to an emotional appreciation of nature's beauty, and artists gave them romantic, poetic interpretations of that subject.

The first landscapes expressed a mood — a dream world of dramatic light and shadow, in which landscape was no longer the background but the center of visual interest. One of the foremost painters of natural landscape was Thomas Cole (1801-1848) of Catskill, who painted great canvasses of the local scenery. His works, as were those of other landscape artists in the group of painters known as "The Hudson River School", were meticulously painted with deep shadow, warm light and delicate mists and grandiose mountains and lakes that lent excitement and glory to the beauty of nature in America. In 1837, Mr. William Van Rensselaer of Albany ordered a pair of pictures from Cole at the cost of $1000 each. The artist, recently returned from England, was enchanted by the past and suggested that the subject matter of these paintings should hark back to the 14th century. He called them *The Departure* and *The Return*. These elaborate allegories depict a knight bidding his lady farewell as he goes off to the wars in early summer. *The Return* shows a sad procession, in autumn, bearing the knight on his litter, dead or dying, back to his lady. Architectural forms such as the Gothic church are used symbolically to conjure up thoughts of the past and religious idealism. In the romantic heyday in which they were painted, they showed moral idealism as well as the consequences of life and the mighty forces of time and nature.

The Return *(1837), oil on canvas, 63" x 39¾", Thomas Cole. Courtesy, Collection of Corcoran Gallery of Art; gift of W. W. Corcoran.*

The Van Rensselaer Manor House was one of two other pictures ordered from Thomas Cole by William Van Rensselaer and his brothers in 1841 at a cost of $500 each, as a gift to their widowed mother to keep as a remembrance of the old home. The painting has an air of nostalgia in the view of the partially hidden house and the lap robe thrown across the empty chair on the lawn. The soft greens and yellows of the foliage lend a glow to the scene. A painting of the Manor House gardens was a companion piece.

Van Rensselaer Manor House *(1841)*, oil on canvas 36" x 24", Thomas Cole. Courtesy, Albany Institute of History and Art.

Timothy Allen Gladding (1818-1864), a portrait and decorative painter, was born in Albany. He and his brother established a house painting and decorating business that was well-known in Albany until after the Civil War. Timothy Gladding also did portrait painting and had a studio at 220 Elm Street, Albany.

The portrait of Mary Ann Keenholts Crounse (1840-1910) is inscribed on the reverse, "Painted by T. A. Gladding, 220 Elm St., Albany, Sept. 1861". Mary Ann was the daughter of James Keenholts, an innkeeper on the Schoharie Plank Road at Knowersville (Altamont), and his wife, Nancy Ogsbury. Farmers from the Schoharie region stayed at the inn during their travels to and from the market at Albany. The inn was built in the early 1830's by Jacob Crounse. It became known as the Keenholts Hotel when it was taken over by James Keenholts.

Mary Ann was painted in the dress she wore for her wedding two years earlier to William Peter Crounse, a farmer of Meadowdale. The fabric of the dress was taffeta and the color was muted green. It is still in the possession of her descendents. Mary Ann's two sisters, Emma and Amelia Keenholts also were painted in 1861 by Timothy Gladding.

Mary Ann Keenholts Crounse *(1861)*, oil on canvas, 26½" x 21½", Timothy A. Gladding. Private collection.

Albany had its own group of painters and sculptors in the mid-19th century. William M. Hart (1823-1891), coming with his family from Scotland to Albany in 1831, started out his career as a window shade and carriage decorator. At this time, there was much rivalry over the decorating of panels for coaches and artists were sought who could make them beautifully ornamental. Hart's work was so praised that, although he was only 18, he decided to attempt portrait painting and, later, landscape painting. He worked here and travelled as far west as Michigan, eventually taking a trip to his native Scotland before returning to Albany in 1841. His landscapes present bright and peaceful aspects of nature. In 1854 he left Albany, to open a studio in New York City.

Scene in the Helderbergs Near Albany, *oil on canvas, 29⅞" x 22"*, William M. Hart. *Courtesy, Albany Institute of History and Art.*

Valley Lands *(1867), oil on canvas, 47½" x 23⅜", James M. Hart. Courtesy, Albany Institute of History and Art.*

William's brother, James McDougal Hart (1828-1901), also painted in Albany and in much the same manner as his brother. His views were mostly of rural scenes and were very restful and familiar. In 1851 he went to Germany for more formal training, returned to Albany in 1852 and joined his brother in New York in 1856. James McDougal Hart, in stating the motive for his paintings said, "I strive to reproduce in my landscapes the feeling produced by the original scenes themselves."[7]

Will H. Low (1853-1932) was an academic painter and a protege of Erastus Dow Palmer. He became well known as an illustrator of periodicals and a mural painter. Some of his decorative work was done for the Albany Savings Bank and his murals are in the State Education Building at Albany. He also became a specialist in the production of stained glass windows for churches. His sketch of a heavily loaded hay wagon, crossing the river on a flat bottom barge, depicts a familiar scene in Albany County in the 19th century.

Haying on the Hudson, *sepia on paper, 14" x 11", Will H. Low. Courtesy, Albany Institute of History and Art.*

117

In early America, wood had been the sculpture medium. By 1830-1840 however, a group of American sculptors were working in Rome and Florence, doing figure sculpture in marble. Their works enjoyed great popularity and they produced some excellent work in a neo-classic style.

Erastus Dow Palmer (1817-1904) was a self-educated man who fully developed a great talent. Leaving school at 12 years of age, he began to work at carpentry, which eventually led him into woodcarving and cabinetry. At the time of his marriage he settled in Utica. While there, he saw carving work on shell cameos and attempted to make a portrait of his wife in this technique. The results were so excellent that he soon was taking orders and turned to cameo cutting as a means of livelihood. The cameo was carved on the shell, from which a series of low relief portraits would be duplicated in plaster for the patron. With these little portraits Palmer began his work as a sculptor. By 1846 he had moved to Albany and in 1848 he modeled a bust of his daughter that was shown at the National Academy of Design in New York. From this show, interest in the work of Palmer began to grow. His career as a producer of marble and bronze busts and statues was to last for a quarter of a century.

Much of Palmer's work was sensitively modeled with a melancholy sweetness and simplicity that appealed to the public of the time and expressed the sentiments of the day. While other sculptors were studying in Italy, Erastus Dow Palmer took his subject matter from the life and legends of America rather than from an imported neo-classical style. The statuary and portrait busts that he produced in his Albany studio achieved national notice. His bronze statue of Chancellor Robert R. Livingston, in which he captured the greatness of the man, was placed in the U.S. Capitol. Locally outstanding are his *Angel of the Sepulchre* at Albany Rural Cemetery and *Faith* at St. Peter's Episcopal Church, Albany. Palmer created the *Angel of the Sepulchre* in 1868 for the memorial to Emma R. T. Banks, who died at age 31 in childbirth. She was the niece of Erastus Corning. The seated Angel is considered one of Palmer's major works and exhibits a commanding presence with a strong, finely modeled face and head and graceful folds to the robe.

Angel of the Sepulchre *(1868), marble, Erastus Dow Palmer.*

A Sculptor's Studio, painted in 1857 by Tompkins Matteson of Albany, depicts the interior of Palmer's studio with several stonecutters at work on various pieces of sculpture. The painting is particularly important because it is a rare depiction of a specific artist at work. Erastus Dow Palmer is in the foreground, wearing a wine colored cap and grey tunic with red draperies in the background. Launt Thompson, his assistant, is at the right of the picture in black costume and Charles Calverly is at the left background. The full length *Indian Maiden* statue is at right rear, the first full length statue made by Palmer. Above the doorway at center is the tablet depicting *Faith*. Tompkins Harrison Matteson (1813-1884) was a historical and genre painter of national and rustic subjects, born in Peterboro, Madison County, N.Y., but in later life he maintained a studio in Albany.

A Sculptor's Studio *(1857), oil on canvas, 37¼" x 29", Tompkins Matteson. Courtesy, Albany Institute of History and Art.*

White Captive *(1858), marble, Erastus Dow Palmer. Courtesy, Metropolitan Museum of Art, New York City. Gift of Hamilton Fish, 1894.*

In January 1858 Palmer wrote that he was busy modeling his finest work, *The White Captive*. Fifteen years earlier the American sculptor Hiram Powers had achieved acclaim for his statue of a young girl entitled *The Greek Slave*. Powers, and other sculptors of his time, felt that their work should express noble sentiment and moral themes. They were greatly influenced by the classical revival and sculpted idealized mythological figures that had a kinship with ancient art. The aloof facial features and the coiffure of *The Greek Slave* are neo-classic in composition.

Erastus Dow Palmer did not borrow an imported style for his *White Captive*, but worked from nature, with no hint of ancient mythology. He chose an American subject for representation in the nude figure of a young white girl snatched from her home and held captive by hostile Indians. Her form, facial features and simple hairdress are American in feeling. Americans could identify with the luckless but brave young woman, and there was great enthusiasm for Palmer's work. He had done the figure with his usual excellent craftsmanship and put emphasis on naturalism and simplicity, which were his hallmarks.

The sculptor William J. Coffee (1774-1846), also listed as a portrait painter, settled in Albany from 1827 to 1845 and executed several bas-reliefs for the City Hall. By 1840 he was making plaster casts for Henry Kirke Brown, who was working as a sculptor in the area. Erastus Dow Palmer probably saw his work in the city. Henry Kirke Brown (1814-1886) began his career by cutting silhouettes and then studying portraiture. By 1839 he left Boston, where he had been producing sculpture, and came to Albany to model Dr. Alonzo Potter of Union College. During his stay in Albany he modelled about 40 busts and was under the patronage of Ezra P. Prentice, owner of the estate *Mount Hope* at Kenwood. In the period in which Brown worked, it was not felt necessary to portray character but only to model likenesses. Naturalism was the dominant style in American sculpture.

Charles Calverly (1833-1914) was born in Albany and apprenticed at an early age in the shop of John Dixon, a marble cutter. At 20, he became an assistant in Erastus Dow Palmer's studio. For 15 years, he remained with Palmer and in 1868 went to New York and set up as a portrait sculptor. He did busts and profile reliefs in both marble and bronze. His statue of the poet, Robert Burns, stands in Washington Park, Albany, and was erected in 1888.

Another apprentice of Erastus Dow Palmer was Launt Thompson (1833-1894). He was born in Ireland and arrived in Albany at age 14, where he worked under Palmer for nine years. While still a young boy he began the study of anatomy with Dr. James Armsby of Albany and he made drawings of bone and muscle structure of the human figure with Dr. Armsby. Palmer undoubtedly recognized the boy's talent, and in turn Thompson was greatly influenced by his master. He was the best known of Palmer's pupils and had a lucrative and accomplished career, but ended his days in complete mental and physical collapse. In 1857 he established his own studio in New York, beginning to do profile portrait work and, later, portrait busts and statues. Especially notable is his bronze statue of Napolean I, and his head of the poet, William Cullen Bryant, now at the Metropolitan Museum.

The harsh reality of strife and bloodshed of the Civil War brought an end to the romantic visions of people and artists alike. New ideas and a change in taste were brought about by the rush for material progress. This was characterized in the last quarter of the century by the new "millionaires" who were ready to hang European paintings on the walls of their pseudo-castles and chateaux mansions. American artists always had looked to Europe as a culture source and many went abroad at this time to study the techniques which were used by the European painters. There was a decline of American painting into sentimentalism and historical anecdotes as subject matter. There were still portrait painters around, but the rapid development of the camera after the War brought about their slow demise. Portraits were painted mainly as a point of prestige. Some American artists painted with objective realism, like Thomas Eakins and Winslow Homer. Others, such as John Singer Sargent, who painted with bold strokes that blended color and motion, with little or no drawing technique, foreshadowed the period of Impressionism in painting that was soon to come to the fore.

Albany County had several artists who achieved prominence during the middle and later part of the 19th century. Homer Dodge Martin (1836-1897) was a self-taught artist except for a two week period when he studied painting and drawing under James M. Hart. He opened his first studio in the mid-1850's in the old museum building at State and Broadway but in 1862 had left for New York City. His paintings had a semi-abstract quality related to others who were painting in an impressionistic manner. He especially was noted for his many Adirondack mountain scenes.

One of Martin's friends was George H. Boughton (1833-1905), a portrait, genre and landscape painter. As a young man in Albany, Boughton sold so many of his works that he was able to take a sketching trip to England at the age of seventeen. By 1861, he returned to Britain where he lived until his death, but even as an expatriate he had many American patrons. His picture studies were taken usually from the life of the American colonists, and his artistic spirit seems to have been formed in America. He also painted many scenes of Breton peasant life, which were very popular in England. There is a soft coloring and wholesome charm to his art as seen in his *View of Albany Near Kenwood.* Perhaps his best known picture nationally is his *Pilgrims Going to Church.*

View of Albany Near Kenwood *(1854) oil on canvas, 56" x 33½", George H. Boughton. Courtesy, Albany Institute of History and Art.*

121

Edward Gay's (1837-1928) view of the Albany County stream *The Normanskill*, reflects him as a painter who tended to be impressionistic. Growing up in Albany, Gay painted landscapes as early as 1856. In later life, he resided in Mt. Vernon, N.Y.

The Normanskill, *oil on canvas, 24⅛″ x 13⅞″, Edward Gay. Courtesy, Albany Institute of History and Art.*

Asa Weston Twitchell (1820-1904) came to Albany from Massachusetts in 1843 and opened a studio on North Pearl Street, where he was listed as a portrait painter. He spent the remainder of his life in Albany and achieved local renown. His self portrait reveals the artist in his working garb at his studio, which was above the Annesley Art Store, well known in its time as a place where artists congregated. Twitchell's residence was on New Scotland Road near Slingerlands.

Self-Portrait, *oil on canvas, 54¼″ x 40⅝″, Asa W. Twitchell. Courtesy, Albany Institute of History and Art.*

The Flight of Night (1878), oil and chalk, 99" x 62", William Morris Hunt. Courtesy, Pennsylvania Academy of Fine Arts.

The Flight of Night by William Morris Hunt (1824-1879) is a preliminary study painted for the ceiling lunettes in the Assembly Chamber of the Capitol at Albany in 1878. The Persian goddess of the waters and fertility, *Anahita*, inspired Hunt to portray her in this allegorical painting which depicts the darkness of ignorance fleeing before the light of civilization. The composition has a dreamlike quality of light and movement, is filled with imaginative poetry and is painted broadly and directly.

William M. Hunt was from a well-to-do family of Brattleboro, Vermont. He studied in Germany and Paris, where he learned a new ideal of vaporous figure painting, expressing subjective feeling through the use of pigment and color. Hunt was influenced by the works of the French painter, Millet and the Barbizon School of painting in France. *The Flight of Night* shows the American imitation of European styles of art. Hunt influenced many American art students to study in Paris rather than in Italy, and this exerted considerable French influence on American taste.

H. H. Richardson had sought Hunt to execute the Capitol murals. They were painted directly upon the stonework and were eventually destroyed by the effect of moisture. The murals were important in that they represented a pioneer venture in the integration of the arts in building construction and decoration in the United States.

Solomon S. Leonard *(1867), oil on canvas, 36" x 24½", Thomas Kirby Van Zandt. Private collection.*

Solomon Southwick Leonard (1811-1884) lived at 8 Delaware Turnpike in 1848 and is so listed in the Albany City Directory for that year. This would have been at the corner of Delaware Turnpike and Lydius Street (Madison Avenue), that in those years was a thinly settled area. We find no mention of his living in Albany or being listed in the directories after 1857. His wife was Angelica LaGrange (1814-1850), a descendent of early settlers on the Normanskill Creek near Albany. Solomon Leonard was descended from Captain John Leonard (1738-1801), born in Wittenberg, Germany. Captain Leonard is recorded as a soldier from Bethlehem, Albany County, who served in the Revolutionary War. We know that Solomon's son, Isaac LaGrange Leonard (1845-1910), lived in Bethlehem along the Delaware Turnpike between Unionville and Adamsville (Delmar), in a fine white farmhouse.

The portrait has descended in the Leonard family and is probably of Solomon Southwick Leonard. It is dated 1867 in the lower left corner and signed "Van Zandt". Mr. Leonard is wearing a black coat with grey trousers and has his feet resting on an orange rug. The horse is chestnut brown and the sky is bathed in a pinkish light. There is a river in the background. Thomas Kirby Van Zandt (1814-1886) was born in Albany and was a noted painter of animals. He maintained a studio on Knox Street at the head of Hudson Avenue, where he executed commissions for local horse fanciers as well as for many wealthy and well-known owners of prize animals. His son, William, also became a noted animal painter. Nineteenth century persons were devoted to the horse, not only for his working abilities, but also for the sense of pleasure he could give in a good trotting race or a swift ride in carriage or cutter.

The Art of Everyday Life

Not everyone could afford or appreciate the works of the academic romanticist painters. Many ordinary people wanted to bring color and beauty into their daily lives and surroundings. Thus, other types of art in a folk or self-taught tradition came into popularity before and during the 19th century.

Genre paintings, such as John Wilson's *State Street*, depicted scenes of daily life in the town and countryside. These scenes tell a story of some phase of human interest or endeavor. While we know about some of the artists who painted in the folk tradition, we know very little about many of those who painted or drew local specimens of art that adorned the walls of Albany County homes.

There were several types of artists who worked in the folk-genre tradition in the 19th century. The professional artists painted and drew pictures as a means of livelihood. Those who worked in the craft tradition painted sleighs, carriages, signs, decorated houses and later turned to painting portraits and scenes. Others were people who had some inclination to artistic endeavors and drew or painted in their spare time, mainly for their own pleasure. Also, young ladies, who had art and needlework instruction in the seminaries and academies, transferred their skills to paper and linen.

What these artists accomplished was not necessarily fine academic art, but the pictures were realistic in detail and vigorous in rendition, and provide a legacy of artistic expression.

The decorative painting from an inn at Potter Hollow shows the impending collision of *The Yosemite and the Charlotte Vanderbilt*. The painting is signed W. W. Cornwell, 1882, and it was found set into the woodwork below the bar of the old inn at Potter Hollow. On the night of July 14, 1882, the steamboat *Charlotte Vanderbilt* was headed downstream on the Hudson when, just north of Esopus Meadows lighthouse, she was struck and sunk by the steam yacht *Yosemite*. The *Yosemite*, making her first trip on the river, was carrying ocean running lights, and the pilot of the *Vanderbilt* misread them to indicate that he was coming up on a boat with two barges in tow. As the two boats rushed toward each other, the pilot of the *Vanderbilt* unaccountably swerved to the left, directly into the path of the *Yosemite*. The *Vanderbilt* was split in two and sank almost immediately, but the *Yosemite* was undamaged and fortunately no lives were lost.

The painting shows us this scene just a few seconds before the collision. On the left, someone has penciled in, but not painted, two barges, in a naive attempt to show us the mysterious cause of the accident. On the riverbank, the lighthouse sends out its beam, the Albany night train speeds south, and people go about their business, all unaware of the impending disaster.

The Yosemite and the Charlotte Vanderbilt *(1882), oil on wood, 18" x 7". W. W. Cornwell. Courtesy, New York State Historical Association, Cooperstown.*

The genre painting by John Wilson depicts State Street in Albany as it looked ca. 1848. Looking west from the intersection of Broadway and State, one can see the Marble Pillars building on the corner, at the right of the scene. This building housed a museum that exhibited natural curiosities, the stage coach offices of Thorpe and Sprague and the victualling house of Nathaniel Adams. Philip Hooker's State Bank and St. Peter's Church are on the right center, with his Capitol at the head of the street. Farmers are vending produce in the middle of State Street. John Wilson was listed as a painter in Albany and lived there between 1844 and 1852.

View of State Street *(ca. 1845), watercolor on paper, 28¼" x 20¼", John Wilson. Courtesy, Albany Institute of History and Art.*

In a farmhouse just outside of the village of Rensselaerville, there are some remarkable wall frescoes done by an unknown artist. The little unpretentious house was built about 140 years ago. It is not usual to find these murals in New York State — they are more frequently found in houses in New England. Some itinerant artist may have come to Rensselaerville in the early years of the 19th century and painted these wall scenes. French scenic design wallpapers were imported during the neo-classic period and this type of free hand painting might have been an attempt to duplicate these expensive papers.

The murals are in the front parlor of the house, which is a small room. The scale of the paintings is too large for the confined space they occupy. The tree trunks are a deep brown and the feathery leaves of the trees are a strong, dark green. All is done in freehand painting on plaster walls. While the drawing is naive, the design and bright colors of the paintings must have given an exotic appearance to the little parlor.

Wall Painting (19th century), Rensselaerville. Unknown artist.

Wall Painting (19th century), Rensselaerville. Unknown artist.

A rural piece of folk art done in bright colored crayon is the sketch that shows the little cabin of an old slave located on the Fox Creek at Berne. The inscription below the picture reads:

"In memory of Jack Dietz and Dinah his wife. Jack was sold as a slave in the year 1792 to John Jost Dietz of the town of Berne: their little cabin was built on the bank of the creek running through Berneville, one mile north of the village. In 1848 Jack died, Robert Ball of Switzkill bought the cabin and contents and this old cabin was jack's, taken from the woodshed loft, by Mrs. A. V. Ball in 1883 as a relic. This poor old slave has gone to rest, I hope that he is free. Disturb him not but let him rest, Down in Berne Cemetery."

Cabin of Jack Dietz (19th century), Berne. Unknown artist. Courtesy, Berne Historical Association.

Campaigns on Capitol Hill

The dominant personalities who had led political parties in the first part of the 19th century were to be supplanted by ideals and beliefs that would shape party unity in later years. The Jacksonian Democrats, encompassing both a conservative group and a radical faction led by Martin Van Buren, dominated Albany politics from 1825-1850. They called themselves the Democratic Republican Party, but soon dropped the Republican and have ever since been known as the *Democratic* party. During these years, another new party, the *Whig*, grew out of many differing political factions, partly from distrust of Jacksonian policies and also in protest against the Masonic order. The Whigs gained control of state government in 1838, under the leadership of Thurlow Weed, and were in and out of power alternately until 1855.

Political maneuvers led to the election of William L. Marcy to the Governorship and Martin Van Buren to the Presidency in 1836, but within a very short time the Albany Regency and its power were destroyed, in large part by the Panic of 1837. The Democrats were held responsible for the problem and turned out of office. At this time, Thurlow Weed became the political power within the State, with the election of the Whig Governor, William H. Seward, whom he supported. By 1846, the people were calling for a revision of the State Constitution. The delegates assembled at Albany and two important ideas were adopted in the new Constitution: a ceiling on state debt and the election rather than the appointment of many officials. The anti-renters also exerted great influence for land reform laws at the convention.

The spectre of slavery raised its head by 1840-50 and the views of Albany County political leaders were made known on a state and national level by meetings, resolutions and legislative messages. By 1854, the Republican party had been formed, partly to prevent the spread of slavery into new territories. Many Whigs joined forces with the Republicans, and made the unification of the two groups complete.

By 1860, William H. Seward, the able senator who often spoke out against the slave system, was at the Repubican national convention, confident that his political helpmate, Thurlow Weed, could secure the nomination for him as the Republican candidate for president. Some New Yorkers, among them Horace Greeley, were opposed to Weed's backing of Seward and joined their efforts with an active group that supported another candidate, Abraham Lincoln. Seward subsequently became Lincoln's Secretary of State and the anti-Weed faction in Albany put forth Horace Greeley as a candidate to take Seward's senate seat. Weed's man, Ira Harris, won the seat and Greeley went back to his *New York Tribune* newspaper.

After the Civil War, the political scene in Albany lost some of its luster as bosses dominated the parties and special interests were patronized. Regional interests often superceded statewide concerns and there was dissension between the governors and the Legislature. Albany County, as the seat of state government, was ablaze with scandals that reached even the national level, with both Democrats and Republicans equally involved. In the latter part of the century, a consortium of able Democratic governors did bring solid achievement in government, and Albany became for one of them, Grover Cleveland, the stepping stone that led to the Presidency. Theodore Roosevelt, another future President, was elected Governor of New York in 1898 on the Republican ticket.

Nicholas Biddle Kittell (1822-1894) painted Governor Marcy in 1857. Kittell was probably born in Kinderhook, N.Y., and may have had a studio in Albany where his plied his trade of portrait painting. William Learned Marcy (1786-1857) came to Troy from Massachusetts to study law, shortly after serving in the War of 1812. Before long, he had removed to Albany and entered the political realm as a Jeffersonian-Republican. He formed an alliance with Martin Van Buren and helped form the Albany Regency. By 1831, he was a U.S. Senator, but resigned to become Governor of New York in 1833, a position which he held for three terms. It was assumed that he was seeking a high federal post and a breach came between him and Van Buren, who was already losing power. President Polk appointed Marcy his Secretary of War during the time that the United States was at war with Mexico. Marcy acquitted himself well in this post and President Pierce named him Secretary of State from 1853-57. William Marcy's public career came to an end when he died suddenly at Ballston, N.Y., on July 4, 1857. He is buried in the Albany Rural Cemetery. under a granite monument designed by Erastus Dow Palmer.

William Learned Marcy *(1857), oil on canvas, 42¼" x 36", Nicholas Biddle Kittell. Courtesy, New-York Historical Society, New York City.*

A President Passes

Chester A. Arthur Monument - Albany Rural Cemetery (1887), Ephraim P. Kaiser.

An assassin's bullet, shot into the body of James A. Garfield in 1881, catapulted Chester Alan Arthur of Albany into the Presidency of the United States.

Chester Arthur (1830-1886), son of the Reverend William Arthur, a Baptist preacher, was graduated from Union College, while his father held a pastorate in Schenectady. The Reverend Mr. Arthur, who came to America from Scotland in 1815, also had served churches in Vermont, Albany, Watervliet and Newtonville. After graduation from college, Chester Arthur taught school at Pownal, Vermont, and in Schaghticoke and Cohoes, N.Y. Both he and James Garfield were teachers in Rensselaer County at about the same time.

By 1853 he had joined a law firm in New York City and during the Civil War he served as State Quartermaster General. After the war, Arthur resumed his law practice and became active in the Republican Party. President Grant appointed him to the position of Collector of the Port of New York in 1871, a federal patronage position. He served in that capacity until 1878, when he was ousted by President Rutherford B. Hayes. Arthur was known as a "spoilsman", and was a prominent figure in the political system run by New York Senator Roscoe Conkling. Party activities revolved around the theory that "to the victor belonged the spoils". These views did not coincide with those who advocated civil service reform, as had been promoted by Presidents Hayes and Garfield, partly to escape from the unsavory aura of the Grant regime.

There were rival Republican factions at the Convention of 1880 and Garfield received the nomination for president, against the wishes of Conkling's following. To appease that group, Garfield selected Chester A. Arthur as his vice-presidential choice. He knew that Arthur had proved himself a good organizer in his other positions and, though he sometimes kept suspect company, there was no evidence that Arthur himself was corrupt. After Garfield's death, Arthur proved to be a much better president than would have been believed. He avoided partisan politics and, to the astonishment of his critics, he established the Civil Service Commission and proved to be a competent administrator.

Because his wife had died in 1880, his sister, Mrs. John McElroy of Albany, assumed the duties of mistress of the White House during his administration. He had hoped to receive the party nomination again in 1884, but there was too much intrigue within the party. Arthur resumed his law practice but in 1886 was forced to retire for reasons of health. He died in November of that year and is buried in the Albany Rural Cemetery, where a group of his friends erected "The Angel of Sorrow" sarcophagus to his memory.

The plain dark granite sarcophagus is highly polished and rests on a lighter colored granite base. At the southwest corner, a bronze Angel of Sorrow is placing a palm leaf on the lid. The memorial was designed by Ephraim P. Keyser (1850-1937), of Baltimore.

Bibliography

"Albany: A Glimpse of an Old Dutch Town". *Harpers New Monthly Magazine*, 1880.

Albany Institute of History and Art. *Hudson Valley Paintings 1700-1750.* Albany, 1959.

Albany, City of. *Albany's Tercentenary.* Albany: J. B. Lyon Co., 1924.

Allen, Edward B. *Early American Wall Paintings 1710-1850.* Watkins Glen: Century House, 1969.

Andrews, Wayne. *American Gothic.* New York: Vintage Books, 1975.

Barker, Elmer Eugene. *The Story of the Ten Broeck Mansion.* Albany: Albany County Historical Association, 1953.

Barnard, Daniel D. *A Discourse on the Life of Stephen Van Rensselaer.* Albany: Hoffman and White, 1839.

Batterberry, Ariane and Michael. *The Pantheon Story of American Art.* New York: Random House, 1976.

Bazin, Germain. *History of Modern Painting.* New York: The Hyperion Press, 1969.

Belknap, Waldron Phoenix Jr. *American Colonial Painting.* Cambridge, Massachusetts: Harvard University Press, 1959.

Bennett, Allison P. *Town of Bethlehem, A Brief History.* Altamont, N.Y.: Enterprise Press, 1970.

Benson, Lee. *The Concept of Jacksonian Democracy.* Princeton, N.J.: Princeton University Press, 1961. Atheneum Reprint, 1964.

Berne Historical Society. *Our Heritage.* Cornwallville, N.Y.: Hope Farm Press, 1977.

Bermingham, Peter. *American Art in the Barbizon Mood.* Washington, D.C.: Smithsonian Institution Press, 1975.

Bishop, Robert. *Folk Painters of America.* New York: E. P. Dutton, 1979.

Black, Mary and Lipman, Jean. *American Folk Painting.* New York: Clarkson N. Potter, Inc., 1966.

Blumenson, John J. G. *Identifying American Architecture.* Nashville, Tennessee: American Assn. for State and Local History, 1977.

Bolton, Theodore and Cortelyou, Irwin F. *Ezra Ames of Albany.* New York: The New-York Historical Society, 1955.

Burchard, John and Bush-Brown, Albert. *The Architecture of America.* Boston, Massachusetts: Little, Brown and Company, 1961.

Burke's Presidential Families of the United States of America. London, 1975.

Carrick, Alice Van Leer. *A History of American Silhouettes.* Rutland, Vermont: Charles E. Tuttle Company, 1968.

Cheyney, Edward P. *The Anti-Rent Agitation in the State of New York 1839-1846.* Philadelphia: University of Pennsylvania. 1887.

Child, Hamilton. *Gazetteer and Business Directory of Albany and Schenectady County, N.Y. for 1870-71.* Syracuse: Journal Office, 1870.

Clarke, John M. *James Hall of Albany.* Albany: 1923.

Cooke, Donald E. *Our Nation's Great Heritage.* Maplewood, New Jersey: Hammond, Inc., 1972.

Christman, Henry. *Tin Horns and Calico.* New York: Henry Holt and Co., 1945.

Coulson, Thomas. *Joseph Henry: His Life and Work.* Princeton, New Jersey, Princeton University Press, 1950.

Corwin, Charles E. *A Manual of the Reformed Church in America.* New York: Board of Publication, R.C.A., 1922.

Craven, Wayne. *Sculpture in America.* New York: Thomas Y. Crowell Co., 1968.

Cunningham, Anna K. *Schuyler Mansion, A Critical Catalog.* Albany: NYS Dept. of Education, 1955.

Dilliard, Maud Esther. *An Album of New Netherland.* New York: Bramhall House, Div. of Clarkson N. Potter, Inc., 1963.

Downing, A. J. *Cottage Residences, Rural Architecture and Landscape Gardening.* Watkins Glen, N.Y.: Library of Victorian Culture, American Life Foundation, 1967. Reissue.

Dreppard, Carl W. *American Pioneer Arts and Artists.* Springfield, Mass: The Pone-Ekbert Company, 1942.

Early, James. *Romanticism and American Architecture.* New York: A.S. Barnes and Co., Inc., 1965.

Eberlein, Harold Donaldson. *The Manors and Historic Homes of the Hudson Valley.* Philadelphia: J. B. Lippincott Co., 1924.

Eberlein, Harold D. and Hubbard, Cortlandt Van Dyke. *American Georgian Architecture.* Bloomington, Indiana: Indiana University Press, 1952.

Eliot, Alexander. *Three Hundred Years of American Painting.* New York: Time, Inc., 1957.

Ellis, David M. "Yankee-Dutch Confrontation in the Albany Area". Reprinted from *New England Quarterly*, Vol. XLV, No. 2, June 1972.

Embler, William J. and Mabel B. *History of Hamilton Union Church.* Altamont, N.Y.: Altamont Enterprise Print, 1974.

Faison, S. Lane. *Art Tours and Detours in New York State.* New York: Random House, Inc., 1964.

Filley, Dorothy M. *Recapturing Wisdom's Valley.* Albany: Albany Institute of History and Art and Town of Colonie, 1975.

Fisher, Leonard Everett. *The Limners.* New York: Franklin Watts, Inc., 1969.

Flexner, James Thomas. *America's Old Masters.* New York: Dover Publications, Inc., 1967. Reprint of 1939 edition.

_____. *Nineteenth Century American Painting.* New York: G. P. Putnam's Sons, 1970.

Fox, Dixon Ryan. *Yankees and Yorkers.* Port Washington, N.Y.: Ira J. Friedman Inc., 1963.

Fuller, Rev. Samuel. *The Early Church in the Helderbergs - Two Sermons.* Andover, Massachusetts: Allen, Morrill and Wardwell, 1843.

Garrett, Wendell D.; Norton, Paul F.; Gowans, Alan; Butler, Joseph T. *The Arts in America, the Nineteenth Century.* New York: Charles Scribner's Sons, 1969.

Giddings, Edward D. *Coeymans and the Past.* Coeymans Tri-Centennial Committee, 1973.

_____ *Collected Notes of Edward D. Giddings.*

Gillon, Edmund V. and Lancaster, Clay. *Victorian Houses - A Treasury of Lesser Known Examples.* New York: Dover Publications, 1973.

Glubok, Shirley. *The Art of Colonial America.* 1970; *The Art of the New American Nation.* 1972; *The Art of America from Jackson to Lincoln.* 1973; *The Art of America in the Golden Age.* 1974. New York: The Macmillan Co.

Gowans, Alan. *Images of American Living.* New York: J. B. Lippincott, Co., 1964.

Gregg, Arthur B. *Early History of the Crounse Family in America.* Altamont, N.Y.: Enterprise Press, 1959.

_____ *Old Hellebergh.* Guilderland Center, N.Y.: Guilderland Historical Society, 1975, Reprint.

Groce, George C. and Wallace, David H. *New-York Historical Society's Dictionary of Artists in America.* New Haven, Connecticut: Yale University Press, 1957.

Hagaman, Howard G. *Lily Among the Thorns.* Grand Rapids, Michigan: Half Moon Press, 1961.

Hamlin, Talbot. *Greek Revival Architecture in America.* New York: Dover Publications, Inc., 1964. Reprint.

Harvard College Library. *H. H. Richardson and His Office.* Catalog for exhibition. Dept. of Printing and Graphic Arts, 1974.

Hastings, Katherine B. *William James of Albany and His Descendents.* 1924 Reprint from N.Y. Genealogical and Biographical Record.

Herz, Carol. *Gerrit Van Zandt of Colonial Albany.* Albany Institute of History and Art Research Paper.

Hills, Frederick S. - Editor. *The Jermain Family.* Albany: Albany Argus Press, 1930.

Hills, Patricia, *The Painter's America.* New York: Praeger Publishers, 1974.

_____ *The Genre Painting of Eastman Johnson.* New York: Garland Publishers, Inc., 1977.

Hislop, Codman. *Eliphalet Nott.* Middletown, Connecticut.: Wesleyan University Press, 1971.

_____ *Albany: Dutch, English and American.* Albany: The Argus Press, 1936.

Historical Sketch of the Burns Statue - Albany: Weed Parsons and Co., 1889.

Hitchcock, Henry Russell. *The Architecture of H. H. Richardson and His Times.* Hamden, Connecticut: Archon Books, 1961.

Holdridge, Barbara and Lawrence E. *Ammi Phillips: Portrait Painter 1788-1865.* New York: Clarkson N. Potter, Inc., 1969.

Howat, John K. *The Hudson River and Its Painters.* New York: Viking Press, 1972.

Howell, G. R. and Tenney, Jonathan. *Bicentennial History of Albany County, New York.* New York: W. W. Munsell and Co., 1886.

Huyck, F. C. and Sons. *Kenwood Mills. A Bit of England in America.* New York: G. Lynn Sumner Co., 1937.

Isham, Samuel and Cortissoz, Royal. *History of American Painting.* New York: The Macmillan Co., 1936.

Jones, E. Alfred. *Old Silver of American Churches.* Letchworth, England: National Society of Colonial Dames of America, 1913.

Kaufmann, Henry J. *The American Fireplace.* New York: Galahad Books, 1972.

Keller, Allan. *Life Along the Hudson.* Tarrytown, N.Y.: Sleepy Hollow Restorations, 1976.

Keller, William A. *White Pine Series of Architectural Monographs.* Vol. 10., No. 4. New York: Marchbanks Press, 1924.

Kenney, Alice P. *Albany: Crossroads of Liberty.* Albany: American Revolution Bi-Centennial Commission, City and County of Albany, 1976.

_____ *The Gansevoorts of Albany.* Syracuse, N.Y.: Syracuse University Press, 1969.

Kimball, Fiske. *American Architecture.* Indianapolis and New York: The Bobbs-Merrill Co., 1928.

Kimball, Sidney Fiske. *Domestic Architecture of the American Colonies and the Early Republic.* New York: Charles Scribners Sons, 1922.

Kimball, Francis P. *The Capital Region of New York State, Vol. I and II.* New York: Lewis Historical Publishing Co., Inc., 1942.

Leonard, Vreeland Y. *The John Leonard Family of Albany County, N.Y.*, 1946. Privately compiled. Copy - New York State Library.

Lipman, Jean and Winchester, Alice. *The Flowering of American Folk Art.* New York: Viking Press, 1974.

Maass, John. *The Gingerbread Age.* New York: Bramhall House, 1957.

Malone, Dumas, editor. *Dictionary of American Biography, Vol II, IV, VI, VII.* New York: Charles Scribner's Sons, 1934.

Masten, Arthur H. *The History of Cohoes, New York.* Albany: Joel Munsell, 1877.

McCaubrey, John W. *American Tradition in Painting.* New York: George Braziller, Inc., 1963.

McGurn, Sharmen Wallace. *The Late Lanscapes of William M. Hunt.* Catalog of University of Maryland Art Dept., Museum Trng. Program, 1976.

Michel, Robin L. "An Architectural History of the Coeymans House - A Thesis - 1974". SUNY at Oneonta.

Miller, John C. *The First Frontier: Life in Colonial America.* New York: Dell Publishing Co., Inc., 1966.

Mumford, Lewis. *Herman Melville.* New York: Harcourt, Brace and Co., 1929.

Munsell, Joel. *Annals of Albany, Vols. 1-10.* Albany: Munsell and Rowland, 1858.

Myers, Bernard S., editor. *Encyclopedia of Painting.* New York: Crown Publishing, Inc., 1955.

New York, State University of. *The American Revolution in New York.* Albany: 1926.

Novak, Barbara. *American Painting in the Nineteenth Century.* New York: Praeger Publishers, 1969.

Parker, Amasa J. *Landmarks of Albany County.* Syracuse, N.Y.: D. Mason and Co., 1897.

Pearson, Jonathan. *Genealogies of the First Settlers of Albany County.* Baltimore, Maryland: Genealogical Publishing Co., Inc., 1872. Reprint, 1976.